AMERICAN
WAR LIBRARY

★ The Persian Gulf War ★

LIFE OF AN AMERICAN SOLDIER

Titles in The American War Library series include:

World War II
Hitler and the Nazis
Kamikazes
Leaders and Generals
Life as a POW
Life of an American Soldier in
  Europe
Strategic Battles in Europe
Strategic Battles in the Pacific
The War at Home
Weapons of War

The Civil War
Leaders of the North and South
Life Among the Soldiers and
  Cavalry
Lincoln and the Abolition of
  Slavery

Strategic Battles
Weapons of War

The Persian Gulf War
Leaders and Generals
Life of an American Soldier
The War Against Iraq
Weapons of War

The Vietnam War
A History of U.S. Involvement
The Home Front: Americans
  Protest the War
Leaders and Generals
Life of an American Soldier
Life as a POW
Weapons of War

AMERICAN
WAR LIBRARY

★ ★ ★ ★

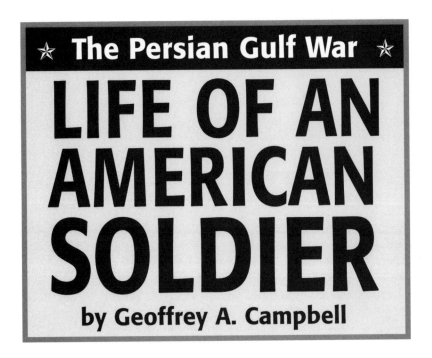

★ **The Persian Gulf War** ★

LIFE OF AN AMERICAN SOLDIER

by Geoffrey A. Campbell

Lucent Books, P.O. Box 289011, San Diego, CA 92198-9011

To Mackenzie and Kirby, and all children, that they
may never have to experience the horror of war

Library of Congress Cataloging-in-Publication Data

Campbell, Geoffrey A.
  Life of an American soldier / by Geoffrey A. Campbell.
     p. cm.—(American war library. Persian Gulf)
Includes bibliographical references and index.
   ISBN 1-56006-713-6 (lib. : alk. paper)
   1. Persian Gulf War, 1991—United States—Juvenile literature.
[1. Persian Gulf War, 1991—Military life. 2. Persian Gulf War, 1991.]
I. Title. II. Series.
  DS79.724 .U6 C36 2001
  956.7044'2373—dc21

                                                      00-010677

Copyright 2001 by Lucent Books, Inc.
P.O. Box 289011, San Diego, California 92198-9011

Printed in the U.S.A.

★ Contents ★

A Nation Forged by War

The United States, like many nations, was forged and defined by war. Despite Benjamin Franklin's opinion that "There never was a good war or a bad peace," the United States owes its very existence to the War of Independence, one to which Franklin wholeheartedly subscribed. The country forged by war in 1776 was tempered and made stronger by the Civil War in the 1860s.

The Texas Revolution, the Mexican-American War, and the Spanish-American War expanded the country's borders and gave it overseas possessions. These wars made the United States a world power, but this status came with a price, as the nation became a key but reluctant player in both World War I and World War II.

Each successive war further defined the country's role on the world stage. Following World War II, U.S. foreign policy redefined itself to focus on the role of defender, not only of the freedom of its own citizens, but also of the freedom of people everywhere. During the cold war that followed World War II until the collapse of the Soviet Union, defending the world meant fighting communism. This goal, manifested in the Korean and Vietnam conflicts, proved elusive, and soured the American public on its achievability. As the United States emerged as the world's sole superpower, American foreign policy has been guided less by national interest and more on protecting international human rights. But as involvement in Somalia and Kosovo prove, this goal has been equally elusive.

As a result, the country's view of itself changed. Bolstered by victories in World Wars I and II, Americans first relished the role of protector. But, as war followed war in a seemingly endless procession, Americans began to doubt their leaders, their motives, and themselves. The Vietnam War especially caused people to question the validity of sending its young people to die in places where they were not particularly wanted and for people who did not seem especially grateful.

While the most obvious changes brought about by America's wars have been geopolitical in nature, many other aspects of society have been touched. War often does not bring about change directly, but acts instead like the catalyst in a chemical reaction, accelerating changes already in progress.

Some of these changes have been societal. The role of women in the United States had been slowly changing, but World War II put thousands into the workforce and into uniform. They might have gone back to being housewives after the war, but equality, once experienced, would not be forgotten.

Likewise, wars have accelerated technological change. The necessity for faster airplanes and a more destructive bomb led to the development of jet planes and nuclear energy. Artificial fibers developed for parachutes in the 1940s were used in the clothing of the 1950s.

Lucent Books' American War Library covers key wars in the development of the nation. Each war is covered in several volumes, to allow for more detail, context, and to provide volumes on often neglected subjects, such as the kamikazes of World War II, or weapons used in the Civil War. As with all Lucent Books, notes, annotated bibliographies, and appendixes such as glossaries give students a launching point for further research. In addition, sidebars and archival photographs enhance the text. Together, each volume in The American War Library will aid students in understanding how America's wars have shaped and changed its politics, economics, and society.

"This Will Not Stand"

On August 2, 1990, Iraqi dictator Saddam Hussein sent hundreds of tanks into neighboring Kuwait. In less than a day, Iraqi forces gained complete control of the small, oil-rich Persian Gulf state. The attack and takeover, made without provocation, drew international outrage. President George Bush vowed, "This will not stand. This will not stand, this aggression against Kuwait." When asked by reporters what he thought the United States could do to get Iraq out of Kuwait, Bush answered, "Just wait. Watch and learn."[1]

Within a matter of months, the United States, as principal partner in an international alliance, had massed nearly half a million troops in Saudi Arabia—Kuwait and Iraq's southern neighbor. In the early morning hours of January 17, 1991, those troops unleashed one of the most one-sided wars the world had ever seen.

Despite the lopsided outcome, the experience of U.S. soldiers in the Persian Gulf was similar to that of soldiers in any war. They knew hardships and homesickness. Most of all, they knew fear. On the eve of the allied ground offensive, Sgt. Robert Langston, who was in a frontline unit, said the possibility of death had made him think about the way he had lived his life: "When I get back, my family will be the most important thing in my life. The uncertainty of whether you come home makes you think of that."[2] Added Sgt. Michael Napier, an antimissile section leader, "We take things for granted. This changes our perspective."[3]

By war's end, Iraq's army had been decimated, and its road and communications networks destroyed. Kuwait had been pillaged, and fleeing Iraqi soldiers had set Kuwaiti oil wells afire and dumped oil into the Persian Gulf, creating an environmental disaster on an unprecedented scale. Thousands of Iraqis and Americans had been forced to confront the horrors of combat, and many paid

An American soldier stands on an Iraqi tank. Though American troops were at a decided advantage over the Iraqis, they were not free of the uncertainty and fear of battle.

the ultimate price—with their lives. A total of 144 Americans died in combat, and 399 were wounded. Unofficial estimates of Iraqi combat deaths range as high as 100,000, although a precise accounting will likely never be made.

Perhaps no one more than a soldier understands the risks and privations of war. And perhaps that is why allied commander H. Norman Schwarzkopf stated to reporters, "Any soldier worth his salt is antiwar."[4]

Chapter 1

"The Army Is Just Like an Anthill"

Within days of Iraq's invasion of Kuwait, U.S. troops began deploying to the Persian Gulf. On August 9, 1990, 2,300 troops from the army's 82nd Airborne Division arrived in Saudi Arabia from Fort Bragg in North Carolina. The 82nd Airborne was just the beginning of what would become a flood of troops and armament from the United States and from U.S. military bases around the world for Operation Desert Shield, the code name used for the defense of Saudi Arabia from possible attack, and Desert Storm, the code name for war waged to force Iraq out of Kuwait.

By November, the United States had placed about 230,000 troops in the Persian Gulf, about half the number of troops the country utilized during the 1960s in the Vietnam War. However, the troop buildup in Vietnam had taken place over several years, whereas the increase in troops in the Gulf took just three months. By the time the war with Iraq was under way, 540,000 American troops were serving in the conflict.

The average American soldier was twenty-seven years old, six years older than the average soldier in the Vietnam War. Most troops in the Vietnam era were conscripted, or drafted into the military for mandatory service. The draft had been ended after the Vietnam War, and the U.S. military in the Persian Gulf War was based on an all-volunteer force of active and reserve troops. The result was an older, more stable force. Nevertheless, like their counterparts in Vietnam, few of the troops deployed to the Persian Gulf had ever experienced battle.

Women and Reserves Played a Large Role

While most of the U.S. troops sent to the Middle East were white males, 137,160, or 25.4 percent, were black and roughly 37,000, or 6.8 percent, were women. Reserve forces, which traditionally had not

American soldiers serving in the Persian Gulf War (pictured) were older and more experienced than troops sent to Vietnam.

been used extensively, also played a large part in the conflict, with 138,343 mobilized for Desert Shield and Desert Storm and 73,431 actually sent into the Gulf region.

Although troops in the reserves knew there was a possibility they could be called to serve in the Persian Gulf, most believed they would not have to go unless they volunteered. Many reservists were attracted to the service because of financial and educational benefits, and considered the probability of going to war slim. For them, service consisted of training one weekend a month and two weeks during the summer, periods during which the so-called cit-

izen soldiers are trained in their appointed tasks.

Belief that they would not be called to active duty was based on a reluctance of past presidents to call on reserve forces. President Lyndon B. Johnson, for example, rejected a mandatory call-up of reserves for service in the Vietnam War, fearing that such a move would be seen around the world as a formal declaration of war. In addition, presidents also worried that a mandatory call-up might lead to a challenge by members of Congress under the 1973 War Powers Act, which among other things requires a president to get congressional approval when armed forces are in battle for more than ninety days.

Reserve Troops Are Mobilized

More than 10,000 reservists volunteered for duty in the Persian Gulf as Desert Shield began, about half of whom were called to active duty because of special skills or training. President Bush, however, knew that more troops would be needed. With the end of the cold war with the Soviet Union, policy makers had decided to trim the size of active forces. Because of the estimated size of the Iraqi army—almost 1 million strong, with 5,000 tanks—the president and military planners knew that a mandatory call-up of reserves would be necessary. On August 22, Bush authorized a mobilization of reserves, and on September 7 the first reserves were deployed. By the end of that month, the army had activated 22,500 reserves, 17,075 of which had not volunteered for service. When this mobilization began, some troops were surprised. One soldier complained, "I didn't come in here to the Army to go to war."[5]

Reserve forces served in a variety of ways, and were particularly crucial in helping U.S. forces prepare to deploy to Saudi Arabia for Desert Shield. On August 5, for example, the 1185th Transportation Terminal Unit, a U.S.

Women made up 6.8 percent of the 540,000 U.S. troops in the Middle East.

Army reserve unit, used its annual two-week training mission to help load the 24th Infantry Division's equipment for deployment to Saudi Arabia.

Another reserve unit, the 136 Airlift Wing of the Texas Air National Guard, helped to deploy troops and equipment ranging from trucks to generators to forklifts. The guard unit had extensive training in the proper loading of aircraft, a necessity to ensure the planes would be properly balanced for flight. "You have to know where everything is going to go in the airplane, or it won't fly," says Sgt. John Grifka, a Gulf War veteran who still serves in the 136 Airlift Wing. "First you load all the equipment so that the plane can keep its center of gravity, and then you just start loading people in any spot you can find. We flew supplies and troops all over the Middle East, carrying everything from toilet paper to missiles."[6]

A Logistical Challenge

Preparations for deployment to the Gulf region took many forms. The first priority was to ready necessary equipment for shipping. In addition, commanders had to make sure soldiers' paperwork was in order while at the same time readying them for possible battle with Iraq. Soldiers who had served during peacetime had to prepare themselves and their families for the possibility of live combat. In addition, because troops were going into the Islamic culture of Saudi Arabia, they had to undergo special sensitivity training. Finally, the troops had to be trained in special desert survival techniques.

Moving Mountains, or Richmond, Virginia

A family moving from one home to another might hire a moving company to help pack and ship its belongings to the new home. When the U.S. Army had to deploy to Saudi Arabia for Operation Desert Shield, it turned to Lt. Gen. William G. Pagonis.

Pagonis was given a daunting task. As he and Jeffrey L. Cruikshank relate in *Moving Mountains: Lessons in Leadership and Logistics from the Gulf War*, "Running logistics for the Gulf War has been compared to transporting the entire population of Alaska, along with their personal belongings, to the other side of the world, on short notice. It has been likened to relocating the city of Richmond, Virginia."

Pagonis was responsible not only for getting troops and equipment to the Persian Gulf but also for making sure the soldiers were fed and that vehicles had adequate fuel once in the Middle East. From August 1990 to August 1991, logisticians for the U.S. armed forces provided more than 122 million meals, the equivalent of feeding every resident of the states of Wyoming and Vermont three meals every day for forty days. Military supply units also provided 1.3 billion gallons of fuel, about the amount used in the District of Columbia, Montana, and North Dakota in a year. Adds Pagonis, "In that same one-year span, those supply units drove almost 52 million miles in the war theater. This is the equivalent of more than 100 round-trips to the moon; or more than 2,000 trips around the world; or more than 10,000 round-trips from Los Angeles to New York."

Readying the massive force for deployment to Saudi Arabia was a logistical challenge. The military had to get 2,000 tanks, 2,200 armored personnel carriers, and 1,700 helicopters to the field, in addition to support vehicles such as trucks and bulldozers, not to mention the troops themselves. American troops and equipment would be sent to the Gulf from bases in the United States as well as Europe, complicating the task of coordinating the buildup. Moreover, heavy vehicles such as tanks could not be sent by airplane, the quickest mode of transportation. Instead, such equipment had to be sent by ship, and sent as quickly as possible because of fears that Iraqi president Saddam Hussein would try to annex Saudi Arabia and gain another 20 percent of the world's oil supply.

Heavy vehicles and supplies could not be sent by airplane and were transported to Saudi Arabia by ship.

Prepositioning Ships Aids Deployment

The United States was able to get initial pieces of heavy equipment to the region quickly because it had earlier assembled three prepositioning ship squadrons in the Atlantic Ocean, the Indian Ocean, and on Guam. The squadrons were established to help the military get heavy equipment to areas requiring military intervention quickly. Each squadron, made up of four or five ships, carried tanks, weapons, and other equipment sufficient to support a sixteen thousand man marine brigade for a month.

The Iraqi invasion of Kuwait, and Bush's decision to block any attempt by Iraq to invade Saudi Arabia, provided the military with an opportunity to test the effectiveness of the squadrons. Soon all were in Saudi Arabia, providing the first U.S. ground troops in the region with the equipment they needed to defend against attack.

Although the prepositioning units helped in getting equipment to the region, much more remained to be done. Deployment required around-the-clock preparations for other units. Equipment including trucks and other heavy vehicles had to be serviced and readied for shipment. Supplies including spare parts, fuel, and oil, also had to be packed. For inland units, much of the preparation involved packing the equipment and supplies for shipment on trains, which delivered it to seaports to be loaded on cargo ships bound for the Persian Gulf.

"Everyone Has a Special Job"

"If you've ever watched ants, that's the way the army is, especially when it's deploying," says Bill Touchette, then a sergeant with the U.S. Army's 515 Transportation Company, which is based in Stuttgart, Germany. "Everyone has a special job, and the work is constant. The army is just like an anthill."[7]

Because the massive amount of equipment and supplies needed to be assembled and shipped quickly, troops had little time off for sleep. Touchette's unit, which would be responsible for providing fuel for armored tanks and helicopters in the event of war, worked twenty-hour-days for two weeks. "When we were preparing to go, we had only four hours off from work at night," he recalls. "We'd get off at midnight and had to be back at work by 4 in the morning. We had two weeks to get ready and get all our stuff on [a train]."[8] Troops spent that working time loading the unit's fifteen fuel tankers and other vehicles and heavy equipment. Once that job was completed, soldiers packed and loaded personal items, such as television sets, video cassette players, and stereo systems.

Troops also had to take the desert environment of Saudi Arabia into account when preparing gear for deployment. Army planners knew that military vehicles would have to be more self-sufficient in the desert than they would be in a lusher, more populated region. As a consequence, troops were ordered to ensure that all vehicles were outfitted with a tool kit, flashlight, reflectors, fire extinguisher, compass, binoculars, maps, communications equipment, shovel, tow rope, and at least five gallons of water for every person in the vehicle. In addition, vehicles were supposed to be equipped with a siphoning hose, air compressor, oil, radiator hoses, fan belts, tape, and air and gas filters.

Operations Were Not Flawless

While military leaders expressed pride in the wide-scale, rapid deployment preparations, mistakes and accidents occurred. The Center for Army Lessons Learned, or CALL, issued a newsletter shortly after the first wave of deployments to the Gulf outlining some shortcomings. For example, the newsletter noted that some equipment was sent to the field well in advance of troops qualified to use it. Other problems arose from the incorrect storage of petroleum, oil, and lubricants. Some containers were damaged because of improper storage, and the newsletter pointed out that some highly flammable fuel was stored with ammunition, a potentially disastrous combination.

In addition, around-the-clock deployment preparations took their toll on troops. The newsletter, titled *Getting to the Desert: De-*

Deployment Had Its Casualties

Even before soldiers faced the dangers of combat and hostile fire in the Persian Gulf War, they were reminded of the dangers of their everyday activities. As the massive U.S.-led military buildup began, troops around the nation readied equipment—and themselves—for deployment to Saudi Arabia.

The rapid mobilization carried significant risk. On December 15, 1990, Carol McKinney, a Missouri National Guard pilot, and two crew members died when the helicopter they were flying to Houston for shipment to Saudi Arabia crashed in a dense fog.

As dangerous as duty could be in the United States, once soldiers reached the Gulf all risks intensified. In all, 375 American men and women lost their lives in the Gulf, 231 of them in non-combat situations. Mobilization proved as dangerous as combat.

---

ployment and Selective Callup Lessons—Desert Shield, 90-11, noted that some accidents in loading equipment could be attributed to a lack of sleep:

Deployment requires continuous operations. Many personnel got very little rest during deployments. Personnel need about 6 hours sleep to sustain operations. Fatigue contributes to human error, the leading cause of Army accidents. Sleep plans must be developed. Leaders must enforce sleep plans to reduce fatigue, prevent accidents and enhance soldier productivity and leader effectiveness.[9]

Another phase of preparation involved more bureaucratic matters. The paperwork process known in the army as Preparation for Overseas Movement, or POM, was designed to get units ready for deployment. Among other things, the POM process involves updating identification cards, shot records, medical and dental records, and pending personnel actions such as court-martial proceedings and security clearances. In addition, officials had to ensure that soldiers' wills were up-to-date. Because of the rapid deployment process, some soldiers arrived for duty without all the proper paperwork, causing delays and backlogs. As a result, the Center for Army Lessons Learned said records should be updated continuously to ensure a higher degree of readiness.

Battle Training Continues

As their records were prepared at the administrative level, the soldiers themselves continued to train for possible war. Some units continued live training exercises. Others preformed walk-throughs of potential battles.

For example, members of Company C of the 2nd Battalion of the 34th Armor in the 1st Brigade of the 1st Infantry Division (Mechanized) from Fort Riley, Kansas, gathered in a classroom to go over the unit's duties in case of war with Iraq. The tank unit would roll into Iraq and clear obstacles for ground troops before going on

An American tank with a plow passes a destroyed Iraqi vehicle. Plows allowed the tanks to clear the path of mines.

to fight Iraqi tanks. On the floor were index cards used to indicate various obstacles the Iraqis were believed, based on intelligence reports, to have placed in the way of a possible American attack. According to reports from defense analysts, the Iraqi troops held positions that were heavily fortified, and troops nicknamed the country "Castle Iraq." The Iraqi border was protected with sand walls, or berms, followed by barbed wire, ditches, minefields, concertina wire, more minefields, more barbed wire, and more concertina wire.

Behind those defenses the military expected trenches filled with Iraqi soldiers.

Second Lt. David J. Russell would lead Company C through the obstacles. His tank would have a plow welded to the front that was supposed to push aside or harmlessly detonate the Iraqi mines. Russell, in effect, would be creating a safe road for the rest of Company C and subsequent troops on foot, to follow into Iraqi territory. However, the duty was a dangerous assignment for Russell that could result in death if a mine exploded into his tank.

"Make Them Convulse Until Death"

During rehearsal Russell indicated he would lead C through the obstacles and then come to a stop at the Iraqi trenches, but Lt. Col. Gregory Fontenot had other ideas: "No! The last thing I want to do is to lose infantry in a fight with a bunch of semiliterate . . . savages. You, you straddle the . . . trench and go! I don't want to fight fair! Make sure nothing there will hurt us! Make them convulse until death!"[10]

What Fontenot was telling Russell to do was bury the Iraqi soldiers. The plow attached to the front of his tank would fill the trenches with soil, eliminating the soldiers as a threat to U.S. infantrymen. Any Iraqis attempting to leave the trenches likely would be crushed by the tank.

Such thoughts as rolling over people with tanks led to soul searching and reflection for some troops. Some were anxious to get to the Persian Gulf and get a taste of battle. Others were more apprehensive, both about the possibility of being killed and the prospect of killing others.

Home-Front Preparations

Even as soldiers prepared to head for the Persian Gulf, the military established special details to provide support services for families of departing soldiers. Made up of soldiers who were not being deployed, the family support units manned toll-free phone lines dedicated to calls for family assistance, provided families with discount ticket books at area merchants, and coordinated donations of nonperishable food items, diapers, baby food, and formula from retailers. In addition, the family support units provided classes for spouses for instruction in the everyday responsibilities that the departing soldier may have ordinarily assumed. Classes included sessions on basic automobile maintenance, home maintenance, plumbing, and checkbook balancing and budgeting.

Soldiers had classes of their own to attend. U.S. military leaders were particularly concerned that the American troops not do anything to offend Saudi Arabians, whose culture is molded by the country's Islamic beliefs. The Muslim religion, for example, prohibits the use of alcohol and drugs, and soldiers were warned by commanders not to attempt to bring such items into Saudi Arabia. Although the military has rules against the use of controlled substances, the stakes are especially high in Islamic nations. "They'll put you to death for doing drugs," Touchette said. "That's the penalty there."[11] The use of alcohol likely would not have been dealt with as severely, but as part of the negotiations with the Saudis the American military leaders promised to keep the troops alcohol-free. Some soldiers did manage to sneak some alcohol with them, but for the most part servicemen and servicewomen strictly followed the no-alcohol policy.

The Do's and Don'ts of Life in Saudi Arabia

Commanders also warned troops against bringing pornography into Saudi Arabia,

Prelude to War

In 1990, the government of the United States was celebrating the end of the so-called cold war with the Soviet Union, and lawmakers on Capitol Hill were examining defense cuts. There was talk in Washington of using the resulting "peace dividend"—the money saved as a result of not having to be prepared for possible war with the Soviet Union—on programs that could help jump-start the economy. The last thing on the minds of most politicians was the possibility of armed conflict in the Persian Gulf. As related by Peter David in *Triumph in the Desert: The Challenge, the Fighting, the Legacy*, Iraqi dictator Saddam Hussein counted on U.S. unpre-

paredness when he ordered Iraqi troops into Kuwait:

> The Iraqi dictator had studied America's experience in Vietnam. What he read convinced him that the American people would no longer go to war unless their own heads were on the chopping block. Shortly before the invasion, he told the American ambassador in Baghdad that "yours is a society that cannot accept 10,000 dead in one battle." He had no such qualms. He had thrown away hundreds of thousands of his own people's lives in a futile war against Iran, and then called it a victory. From the presidential palace in Baghdad, the idea that the United States would risk a bloody war in the desert for the sake of liberating a tiny Middle Eastern emirate made no sense at all.

On August 2, 1990, Iraq invaded Kuwait. Saddam Hussein claimed that Kuwait had been stolen from Iraq by British colonialists, and his army's action was merely an effort to regain what had been taken by others. Hussein counted on the United States to ignore the annexation of Kuwait. Instead, the invasion triggered the largest and fastest military buildup in history.

Saddam Hussein believed the United States would not risk a war over his invasion of Kuwait.

where such materials are considered highly offensive. Saudi women do not appear in public without veils over their faces and clothing that covers their arms and legs, so some American troops were warned against bringing seemingly innocuous pictures with them. For example, a captain in Company C gave a strict interpretation of the no-pornography rule: "A girl in a string bikini's pornography. A girl or a *wife* in shorts is pornography." Holding up a copy of a J. C. Penney catalog open to a page showing a woman modeling a bra, the captain continued, "This is pornography, don't take it to Saudi."[12]

Troops were urged to avoid a number of other things, seemingly innocent to those outside of Islamic culture. For example, they were told not to show their palms or the soles of their feet to native Saudis, who consider such acts rude. Because of the Muslim belief in a paradise that is white, troops were instructed not to pack white underwear.

A hand gesture commonly interpreted in the Western world to mean "everything is okay," formed by curling the index finger to the thumb in the shape of an O, is highly offensive in the Islamic world. Even the customary use of the right hand to shake in greeting was off-limits in Saudi Arabia, because the right hand is commonly used to cleanse oneself after a bowel movement. Troops were also reminded of the impoliteness of pointing, a gesture considered particularly rude in Saudi Arabia because that is the way people there get the attention of their dogs.

Soldiers departing for the Persian Gulf were even given instructions from officers on how to hold conversations with Saudi natives. For example, troops were told they should avoid asking Arabs personal questions, and should never ask questions about the women of an Arab

family because such interest is seen as inappropriate. Soldiers also were cautioned that Arabs typically stand very close to one another while talking, closer than most Westerners find comfortable. Nevertheless, soldiers were instructed not to back away, which would be seen as a sign of rudeness.

A Saudi Arabian woman wears a black veil. U.S. soldiers were given much instruction about the culture of their Muslim hosts.

"You Just Want to Get Going"

In addition to schooling on Islamic mores, soldiers also received instruction on surviving in the desert. Because military leaders had assumed for years that the most likely theater for battle would be in Europe against the forces of the Soviet Union, many soldiers had not been trained for desert duty. Training and instruction covered a wide range of topics, from vehicle tire care to the importance of wearing eye protection such as sunglasses and goggles. Soldiers also were reminded while in the desert to check all clothing for spiders, centipedes, and scorpions before dressing.

Troops also received instruction on building a make-shift compass in case they became lost in the desert. To make the compass, the soldiers were told to place a stick in the ground and to lay a rock at the end of the stick's shadow. After waiting fifteen minutes, they were to draw a line from the rock to the new end of the shadow. The resulting line represents the east-west line.

The packing and the training sessions were as intensive as they were extensive. From the time soldiers were told they would be heading for Saudi Arabia to the time they actually left was generally no more than a few weeks. As preparations wound down, and mobilization neared, soldiers became restless. "After awhile, you just want to get going," Touchette says. "You're ready and you want to go."[13]

Chapter 2

"It Was Home"

For most soldiers headed to the Middle East, Dhahran, Saudi Arabia, was their first stop. Nestled along the Persian Gulf southeast of Kuwait and Iraq, Dhahran became a military terminal in August 1990, with soldiers arriving from the United States and Europe and then heading out to strategic points throughout the Saudi desert.

The soldiers were sent to Saudi Arabia because of fears that an aggressive Iraq would attempt to invade that nation as well as Kuwait and gain an even larger percentage of the world's oil supply. As they arrived in Saudi Arabia, the soldiers knew they could find themselves under attack at any time. They also knew that, even if Iraq did not attack, there was a very real possibility that they could find themselves in battle, especially if Iraq's troops refused to leave Kuwait. Soldiers knew it would be their job to force Iraq out of Kuwait.

The soldiers' introduction to Saudi Arabia was chaotic as jets and cargo planes

continuously landed and took off. Many, especially those who made the nearly twenty-four-hour air trip from the United States in cargo bays, felt stunned by the long ride in military transport planes, and their ears rang from the incessant roar of the planes' engines. Vehicles carrying pallets of equipment and supplies were on the move between the planes and dock areas. Tents were set up to provide some shelter from the blistering daytime sun, but soldiers could find little relief from the constantly blowing sand.

In this terrain of ever-present sand, soldiers in the Persian Gulf wore desert camouflage uniforms in fabric of mixed colors of tan, brown, and black instead of the more familiar olive green battle dress. Soldiers called the desert uniforms "chocolate chips" because of their coloring. Tanks, such as the M1A1, along with Bradley fighting vehicles and other transport vehicles, also were painted to blend into the desert landscape. Some tanks and

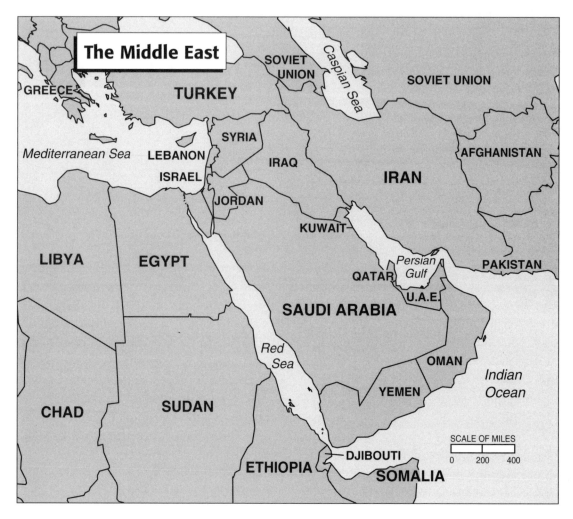

The Middle East

other military vehicles, including the high-mobility, multipurpose wheeled vehicles known as Humvees, arrived in the Persian Gulf painted green, and had to be repainted in what soldiers dubbed "tanning salons" so they would not be easily visible to the Iraqis. Lt. Gen. William G. Pagonis of the U.S. Army's 22nd Support Command believed such efforts were necessary for morale: "Most of my soldiers were aware that a layer of oil, covered with a mixture of sand and water, would have concealed the green paint as effectively, but we saw and took an opportunity to give our combat troops—our customers—an important psychological boost."[14] Pagonis knew that taking the trouble and expense to paint the vehicles would send a strong signal that the military would not cut corners in its support of the troops.

Water Was Essential

Many soldiers waited in Dhahran only a few hours before being dispatched to locations throughout Saudi Arabia. They used the time to relax after their long journey from the United States, lounging in tents or makeshift rest areas in corners of military warehouses, playing cards, talking, and taking naps. Some wrote letters to loved ones at home or snacked on crackers and warm soda. They also received constant reminders to drink plenty of water because of the very real danger of dehydration in the hot, windy climate. "Over there, you reminded people

Mail Call

To the men and women who deployed to the Persian Gulf, nothing broke up their fear and boredom like mail from friends, family, and even strangers. Capt. Keith Rosenkranz in *Vipers in the Storm: Diary of a Gulf War Fighter Pilot* recalls how mail from home vastly improved morale.

One day Rosenkranz was pleasantly surprised to receive packages from his wife and from a good friend. The friend's package included granola and other snacks, along with

> thirty letters written by students in a fifth grade class at Webster Elementary, Malibu, California. I was touched that a group of kids who didn't know me would take the time to write. For the next hour, I sat in the club and read each of the letters. The kids wrote about their school and the different activities they were interested in. Of course, everyone wanted to know what it was like to fly an F-16 and whether or not there would be a war. Most of the boys said they wanted to be pilots some day, and many of them drew pictures of the different jets they wanted to fly. After finishing the last letter, I decided to write a personal note to every child.

Sometimes, however, letters from home would bring sadness because they reinforced the distance between soldiers and loved ones. After reading the letters from the fifth-grade students, Rosenkranz opened the package from his wife. In it were candy and gum, laundry detergent, razors, issues of *Sports Illustrated*, and two letters from his wife "with pictures of her and [our daughters]. The photos of Candice and Kristen were taken just before I left for the Gulf. Each girl took turns wearing my flight cap and . . . scarf while standing in my combat boots. They were so excited to dress up like their daddy. I stared at the pictures, wishing I could relive the moment again."

Mail from home was a valued morale boost for American soldiers.

to take a drink of water when you saw them," one soldier recalls. "You said that instead of saying 'hello.'"[15]

Other soldiers, particularly those in units that relied on many pieces of heavy equipment, had to stay in Dhahran several days as they awaited arrival of their equipment by sea. They were given guidance on what to pack in their duffel bags so they could pass the waiting time in relative comfort. Among other things, the soldiers were advised to pack sleeping bags.

The U.S. Army's 515 Transportation Company, which would be responsible for providing fuel for tanks and helicopters in the event of war, deployed to Saudi Arabia in December, and was one of the units that remained in Dhahran for a few days waiting for equipment. Some soldiers in the 515 believed that, although it was December, Saudi Arabia would be hot, and consequently, had decided to have their sleeping bags shipped over, leaving more room in their duffel bags for personal items such as personal cassette players and video cameras.

The company set up open-air cots at the port of Dhahran. As anticipated, the temperature was extremely hot during the day, but once the sun set temperatures dipped. "There's always somebody who thinks he knows everything, but those guys that shipped their sleeping bags found out they made a mistake in a hurry. Those guys were freezing. Some of them had to sleep in empty boxes to try to stay warm. I know I hated to crawl out of my sleeping bag in the morning,"[16] one soldier recalls.

Once in possession of their machinery, the units headed out to set up camp in the harsh Saudi desert. Driving hundreds of miles, often off-road, through the desert, very few soldiers had any idea where they were or where they were going. They simply followed the vehicle in front of them over the hard, dusty, rocky ground until the convoy came to a halt at what would become their unit's camp sites.

Conditions were primitive initially. Some soldiers set up tents on the moonlike terrain and draped them with camouflage netting to make the camps less visible from the air, while others bulldozed protective berms, or walls of earth, at the perimeter of the camp. Soldiers also laid concertina wire around the camps, another means to slow any potential advance by Iraqi soldiers. Another high-priority item in establishing the camps was to build bunkers to protect soldiers in the case of an Iraqi missile attack.

Fear of Scud Missile Attacks

Each platoon was responsible for building its own bunker. A hole was bulldozed in the rock-hard ground, and then soldiers filled sandbag after sandbag. A plywood roof was set over the hole and then covered by sandbags and dirt. Sandbags also shored up the sides of the bunker. Once completed, the bunkers could hold about sixteen people, but not in great comfort. Although the

Soldiers wear chemical-protection gear while sitting in their bunker, a shelter designed to protect them from missile attack.

bunkers provided a haven in case of attack, they also reinforced to soldiers the reality of warfare and the death and destruction that could await them.

One of the most feared missiles in Iraq's arsenal was the so-called Scud missile, which weighed 14,000 pounds and could travel up to 180 miles. Developed by the Soviet Union in the 1960s, the Scud missile was a direct descendant of the German V-2 rocket that terrorized Great Britain in World War II because of its brutal unpredictability. Although, like the V-2, the Scud was highly inaccurate, it was feared by soldiers because it struck the

ground with great force, and because of fears that Scud missiles may have been modified to carry chemical weapons.

Iraq had a stockpile of somewhere between 2,000 and 4,000 tons of chemical weapons, the use of which could cause an agonizing death. Iraq's arsenal included mustard gas, which was first used during World War I. Mustard gas can cause blindness and burn skin, making victims susceptible to further attack by other chemical agents, such as nerve gases. It also can sear lungs if inhaled, leading to an excruciating death.

Iraq also possessed nerve gases, which were initially developed in World War II. Nerve gas works by attacking the central nervous system of victims, causing convulsions, paralysis, and death. Nerve gas enters the body primarily by absorption through exposed skin. During its war with Iran, Iraq had increased the lethality of nerve gas by combining it with mustard gas. The mustard gas blistered the skin of victims, making the skin more vulnerable to the absorption of nerve gas agents.

Protective Clothing

In addition, Iraq had weapons that released hydrogen cyanide gas, which can cause suffocation by preventing oxygen from getting into a person's lungs. Hydrogen cyanide gas also can deactivate the filtering agents in gas masks and other filters, rendering them useless to the wearer.

Each soldier was outfitted with a gas-proof suit for protection against chemical weapons. In addition to a gas mask, which provided protection for the wearer's face and lungs, the suits included a chemical protection overgarment, to which chemical detection tape was fastened near the wrist of the garment. If chemical weapons were used, the tape would change colors, alerting soldiers to the danger. Soldiers also carried an antidote for nerve gas.

Fear of possible chemical attack affected soldiers in different ways. Some be-

came nonchalant about the frequent gas-attack warnings that filled the desert air, while others became paralyzed with fear. Often the gas warnings were drills, but sometimes chemical sensors surrounding the camps were set off, sometimes by nothing more lethal than a urinating camel. Other times, warnings were sounded when radar detected the launch of Scud missiles. Wearing the gas-proof suits, including gas masks, heightened feelings of claustrophobia among some soldiers, especially in the close quarters of the bunkers. At times, soldiers stayed in the bunkers for half an hour or longer, until it became clear that the camps were not in danger. Coupled with the jangled nerves of being almost constantly in danger from possible Iraqi attack, it was not uncommon for soldiers to vomit in their masks. "But you had to keep them on, just in case,"[17] soldier Bill Touchette said.

Sgt. Carla Barbour-Clark of the 438th Aerial Port Squadron was a forklift operator moving pallets at an air base in Saudi Arabia. She said she never became accustomed to the all-too-common threat of Scud missiles as she worked: "That rush of adrenaline comes, and there's a moment of panic. I don my chem gear, and if I see someone who is having trouble with theirs, I help them."[18]

"We Were Expecting Casualties"

One soldier recalls being roused from sleep by a gas attack alert at about 2 A.M. Members of the unit hastily put on their

Preparing for the Worst

By mid-January 1991, U.S. and coalition forces were dug into positions in Saudi Arabia, making final preparations for the possibility of war. Those preparations included provisions for the handling of casualties.

Retired Maj. Gen. Jeanne Holm of the U.S. Air Force notes in *Women in the Military: An Unfinished Revolution* that preparations were colored by concerns over the potential use of chemical or biological weapons by Iraq: "Protective masks and clothing (called 'chem gear') were issued to all the troops and kept close at hand. Medical personnel were trained to set up temporary facilities to decontaminate and treat victims. 'Everyone knows what to do and knows how to do it, but they have never done it for real,' a Navy official said."

Iraqi dictator Saddam Hussein had already used such weapons on ethnic groups in his own country, and against the Iranians in the 1980–1988 war between the two nations. And he promised to use them again, this time against U.S.-led forces, if the coalition attacked Iraq.

gas-proof suits and headed for their bunker. But unknown to the rest of the unit, a woman had passed out on the floor of her tent, overwhelmed by fear. When the welcome all-clear alert was sounded, the woman was found on the floor of her tent, still passed out.

The frequent alerts reminded soldiers how close they were to actual combat, and the activation of two hospital ships, the *Mercy* and the *Comfort*, sent a clear signal to soldiers—and Iraq—that the growing U.S. military presence was not a hollow show of force. "These ships were a tremendous signal that no bluff was involved. It meant that we were expecting casualties,"[19] says Vice Adm. Frank Donovan, commander of the Military Sealift Command. The *Mercy* and the *Comfort* were equipped to deal with chemical warfare casualties, and together had 24 operating rooms, 8 X-ray rooms, and space for 160 intensive-care patients and 2,000 others.

That message was made even clearer when Seabee, or naval construction, units built the Naval Fleet Hospital at Al Jubayl, a port city on the Persian Gulf, under less than ideal conditions. Deborah Sheehan, a crane operator for a Seabee unit, later recalled the long hours and constant danger of the work:

> We worked twelve hours on, twelve off. What we were offloading mostly was ammo, vehicles, tents, supplies for the fleet hospital at Al Jubayl. . . . While on the pier, we were under attack by Scuds. One blew up over the warehouse while we were unloading some ammo.[20]

Training and More Training

In addition to making camps, building needed facilities, and keeping a watchful eye out for a possible Iraqi attack, soldiers spent a large part of their time in training exercises. Soldiers drilled for hours, laden with their gas-proof suits and full packs in temperatures that reached 120 degrees Fahrenheit. By midmorning the sand beneath soldiers' feet could feel as though it were burning through the soles of their shoes.

As part of combat drills, soldiers made sure all their equipment was working properly. One especially important piece of equipment was the GPS, or Global Positioning System, a handheld satellite communications system that allowed soldiers to precisely identify their position, a must in the featureless desert landscape. It was essential that soldiers knew their position and those of their comrades, in order to avoid firing on fellow American or allied troops. Soldiers had to be particularly careful working with the GPS because the fine desert dust could disable the equipment. Using the GPS in drills gave soldiers the opportunity to test the system under the harsh desert conditions.

As they continued to drill, combat troops grew restless. Although there was speculation that the United States and its allies would rely mostly upon air strikes in an offensive battle against Iraq, ground troops knew that to win a war, their efforts would be paramount. Asked by reporters whether it would be possible to win a war against Iraq solely by utilizing bombers and fighter jets, Sgt. Dee Crane, a Vietnam War veteran, answered:

> The only ground you hold in a war is the ground an infantry soldier is standing on. You don't hold territory by flying over it and dropping bombs on it. All that can do is make the ter-

ritory dangerous for your enemy, and as soon as you *stop* bombing it, he's back. To *win* a war, you have to control the land, and that means infantry. Sooner or later, a grunt has to go in and take it for you.[21]

Truck Stops and Wolfmobiles

Supplies and equipment were continually on the move during Desert Shield, and for the soldiers who drove trucks throughout Saudi Arabia, the duty could be extremely hazardous because of a sometimes primitive road system and heavy traffic. Drivers often were at the wheel eighteen hours a day, transporting tons of dangerous cargo. The army's 22nd Support Command had already planned on building fuel and maintenance centers where drivers could refuel and vehicles could be serviced, but soon decided to create centers similar to the truck stops that line highways in the United States. Outfitted with shower facilities, a lounge to take naps in or watch television and fast food such as hamburgers, the centers provided rest areas for the drivers. "It's clear that we made the lives of our drivers safer and better. They were more alert, and also more safety conscious in general,"[22] says Pagonis. The success of the centers led planners to consider the possibility of providing hamburgers and fries to frontline troops.

Pagonis told Chief Warrant Officer Wesley Wolf to come up with a plan for mobile canteen trucks that would serve the camps set up by combat troops throughout the Saudi desert. He developed vehicles that came to be known as "Wolfmobiles," named in Wolf's honor. Pagonis says the relatively simple project produced significant results:

Imagine that you've been at some remote and desolate desert site for weeks, or even months, consuming dehydrated or vacuum-packed military rations. One day, unannounced, an odd-looking vehicle with the word "Wolfmobile" painted on it comes driving into your camp. The side panels open up, and a smiling crew inside offers to cook you a hamburger to order. "Side of fries? How about a Coke?" Morale shot up everywhere the Wolfmobiles pulled in—a little bit of home in the desert.[23]

Camp Life

When soldiers were off duty, they did the best they could to cleanse themselves of the grit and sand of the Saudi desert. Initially,

In order to sustain the hundreds of thousands of soldiers, trucks hauling supplies and equipment were continually on the move.

they utilized small plastic wash tubs to give themselves sponge baths.

Soldiers also used the small tubs to wash their laundry. To clean their clothes, soldiers put a small amount of detergent in a tub, filled it with water and laundry and then agitated it by hand. Another tub was filled with water for rinsing the garments. Clothes were then hung to air dry.

Eventually, soldiers erected shower facilities in the desert camps. Water for the showers was trucked to the camps in large tankers by support troops. Small buildings made of wood were constructed with deck-like floors built slightly off the ground. Wa-

ter tanks were placed over the units, emptying to spigots that were opened by pulling a chain. Because it got cold in the evening, the water was heated, though many soldiers had to settle for cold showers.

Restroom facilities were rustic but ingenious. They did not, however, afford soldiers much privacy. "Once you got out there, you could forget about privacy,"[24] says Bill Touchette. The latrines were built

---

A soldier's ability to maintain personal hygiene in the field under battle conditions often required adapting military equipment, such as helmets, to uses not envisioned by its designers.

Keeping, and Passing, Time in the Desert

Soldiers in the Persian Gulf kept up a tradition nearly as old as armies themselves. As they waited in the Saudi desert for the possibility of war, they drilled and trained and tried to keep in shape. Many units ran a few miles after breakfast, usually in formation while a platoon leader barked out a cadence.

A cadence is a short poem that serves as a sort of metronome for the soldiers. Carsten Stroud, in *Iron Bravo: Hearts, Minds, and Sergeants in the U.S. Army,* relates a cadence popular with some infantry soldiers:

These days the troops liked the one that ran, "If I die in a combat zone, box me up and ship me home, pin my medals on my chest, tell my mom I done my best, bury my body six feet down, till you hear it hit the ground"— actually a Marine cadence, but it seemed to catch the spirit of the place—and Baker Company would stretch out in a long gray line, shuffling and rolling over the hard ocher dust while the tankers fired up their Abramses in the armor parks and the smell of kerosene and . . . fuel rose up into the morning sky.

like an outhouse, featuring three seats placed over a pit. The waste went into the bottoms of large barrels that were placed beneath the seats, and a trapdoor was built in back to allow the barrel bottoms to be removed for waste disposal. As in all camps, latrine duty was one of the most despised duties for soldiers. Once full, the barrels were taken to a nearby pit. The contents were saturated with diesel fuel and mixed thoroughly, and then set on fire. The waste was burned to keep the camps sanitary. After the wastes had been burned off and the barrels cooled, they were reinstalled below the latrines.

On a Constant State of Alert

When not on duty, soldiers took naps and wrote letters to loved ones. But they never lost sight of the potential for danger. Each soldier had an M-16 rifle and 180 rounds of ammunition ready to respond to warning sirens at any time. One siren signaled a pos-sible Scud attack, another a possible gas attack. Each sent the troops scrambling for their bunkers. Still another alert sounded when the encampment was being approached, and troops had to hustle to the camp's perimeter with weapons in hand. Usually, the alarm turned out to be a sheepherder or some camels, but the soldiers never knew what to expect.

Mail was especially important to the troops, providing a link between them and loved ones back in the United States. But even mail from strangers was welcome. Newspaper advice columnist Ann Landers began a campaign urging Americans to write letters of support to soldiers, a call that was so successful that letters to "any soldier" amounted to 500 tons, or one million pounds a day. The military postal support staff in the Gulf increased from thirteen to thirteen thousand full-time personnel, who distributed more than 70 million pounds of mail.

Soldiers sit near boxes of MREs for shelter as they cover their faces and wait out a sandstorm, or shamal.

One soldier recalls, "A lot of mail would come just addressed to 'Any American Soldier.' We'd grab a couple, read them, and write back, and usually you'd end up writing back and forth. A lot of it came from kids, and that was pretty cool. You'd write them and they'd write back to you."[25]

Soldiers also appreciated receiving packages full of items that were scarce in Saudi Arabia. Especially prized were moist towelettes, sanitary napkins, and batteries, though soldiers also enjoyed the gum and snacks sent by friends and well-wishers.

The tents that soldiers called home could fit about twelve people, though most held only about five. Within a short time the desert homes resembled college dorm rooms, cluttered with empty water bottles and other debris. Soldiers set up coffee pots, televisions, VCRs, and stereos. Some even built entertainment centers to hold electronic components, which were powered by the camp's gas-powered generators. Each tent included gas-fueled potbelly stoves, and tent fires were not uncommon. Laundry was hung to dry both inside and outside the tents.

"All You Can Do Is Stand in It"

Dust and persistent winds were a constant irritant. Even with all the tent flaps closed, a sand as fine as talcum powder coated everything inside the tents. Soldiers covered their sleeping bags with plastic during the day, and by night found that their bedding was still covered with Saudi dust. Weapons had to be cleaned of dust daily to ensure they remained in working order. Sometimes soldiers had to endure intense sandstorms, called *shamals*, which could bring all activity to a halt. One officer said a *shamal* "hits you like a rock. All you can do is stand in it. There's no place to go."[26]

Although living quarters were messy, soldiers were expected to strictly adhere to regulation in their appearance. Soldiers were required to keep their hair cut, and a soldier with electric clippers could expect a steady stream of customers. Women were allowed to wear their hair longer than the men, provided it was tucked underneath their caps.

Food also was a constant concern. Troops generally got at least one hot meal a day, usually eggs for breakfast. Most commonly, soldiers ate so-called MREs, or meals, ready to eat, which were packed in plastic pouches. Typical entrees included "Ham Slices in Natural Juices" and "Meatballs in Spicy Tomato Sauce." Side dishes included items such as potatoes au gratin. Soldiers also received snacks such as M&Ms and cookies. In addition, soldiers got cocoa, which they mixed in coffee for a drink they called "Coco-Joe," and Kool-Aid packets they mixed in their ever-present water bottles.

Sometimes the soldiers had to make do with a small can of pasta, such as those marketed for take-from-home school lunches, a cup of applesauce, and a six-ounce soft drink. But soldiers sometimes enjoyed fresh foods, including pita bread and produce, which were provided by a Saudi food producer and paid for by the Saudi government.

Leisure-time activities also drew soldiers' interests, and camps often sported volleyball courts and baseball diamonds. Troops even arranged pickup football games and constructed small, makeshift, swimming pools in their desert camps. Soldiers sometimes captured desert lizards and organized lizard races, anything to pass the time as they waited for possible battle. To combat troops, the waiting was almost as bad as the reality of war, and at least during Operation Desert Shield, boredom was the primary enemy.

Camp life was unpleasant in many ways, but the soldiers soon got used to the inconveniences of living in the desert. As one soldier put it, "The first day or two, you want to go home. After that, it was home."[27]

Chapter 3

"I Would Trust Her to Cover My Back . . ."

O n March 2, 1991, U.S. Secretary of Defense Richard Cheney took time to sum up the performance of women in the Persian Gulf War: "Women have made a major contribution to this [war] effort. We could not have won without them."[28] The reason Cheney felt the need to single out women in the conflict was the fact that women were for the first time a major part of America's war effort. Never in the history of the United States had so many women—roughly 37,000—gone to war. Although prohibited from serving in combat, they faced many of the same dangers and shared the same hardships as their fellow servicemen.

They also faced many unique problems. The mere sight of women toting guns offended many Saudis. In Saudi Arabia, women are prohibited from driving automobiles or even baring their faces in public. Saudi women never wear shorts in public and are prohibited from working with men. Some Saudi women even wear gloves to avoid any unwanted skin contact with men. Women accompanying men in public walk twelve steps behind in the heavily male-dominated culture.

It did not take long for these ingrained customs to come in sharp conflict with the highly visible U.S. military women. One day in December, Sgt. Dee Crane was in a Saudi city on business when he saw a woman from the 24th Infantry. She was outfitted in full battle dress uniform, or BDU as the soldiers called it, and carrying the ever-present M-16 rifle. Two Muslims spat in her face, and Crane chased them away. "Why the *hell* are we putting up with these [people]?" the soldier asked Crane. "I don't see why we have to put up with all this . . . no beer, they get to spit on me, and all we can do is say, 'Hey, thank you for the privilege of allowing us to die for your . . . country.'"[29]

A Clash of Cultures

Such incidents were far from uncommon, especially in the early stages of Desert

Shield. One day a group of men and women soldiers were sent into the city of Ad Dammam to set up a medical supply center. As the temperature rose, the soldiers worked in T-shirts with their sleeves rolled up. Residents complained to religious officials about the women's exposed arms, and the women were subject to insults from passersby. A colonel in the Saudi military explained that the sight of women with their sleeves rolled up was offensive to devout Muslims because they considered it an obscene display of human flesh. Despite the heat, U.S. military leaders quickly required all soldiers working in that area to wear long-sleeved shirts.

They decided it would be unfair to the women soldiers if only the men could wear short sleeves.

The incidents did not go unnoticed in the United States, either. "Women are living a much harder life than the men because of these restrictions. If they can do their jobs under these conditions, they can do their jobs anywhere,"[30] said Rep. Pat Schroeder, a Colorado Democrat then serving as a senior member of the House Armed Services Committee.

Many Saudis were offended by the sight of women carrying guns.

Even before they reached Saudi Arabia, U.S. military women had to endure intense scrutiny. Part of the scrutiny was internal, as many within the military establishment questioned American reliance on reserve forces, in which many women were active. Others, however, saw the situation in the Middle East as an opportunity. Stephen M. Duncan, then assistant secretary of defense for reserve affairs, says, "I knew that all across the land, men and women in thousands of offices, shops, classrooms, clinics,

and firehouses would soon and suddenly be pulled away from their civilian jobs, their families, and their many civilian pursuits, to don the battle dress uniform. Now a new myth had to be challenged—the myth that these part-time soldiers were not prepared for their forthcoming ordeal."[31]

Dual-Service Military Families

Nevertheless, the dramatic increase in the number of women in the military, both active and reserve, created new problems. As Duncan recalls:

> One unusual problem was already causing hardships in reserve families. As greater numbers of women entered the armed forces in recent years, a new social phenomenon had become increasingly common—the dual-service military family. For thousands of couples, reserve service by one spouse while the other pursued an active military career was attractive financially and in other ways. Despite instructions to make provision for the care of children in the event of a reserve activation, however, many families had not. As more and more reservists were activated, pressures on the Pentagon to establish broad policies limiting active service to one family member increased rapidly. To his credit, [Defense Secretary] Cheney did not budge. Across-the-board polices would not be adopted. Reservists who had been paid to be ready when the nation called would be presumed to be eli-

---

Women with Guns

Although women generally were barred from serving in positions close to the front lines, their work assignments often took them to frontline positions. Many women serving in support units, for example, routinely drove trucks to resupply frontline units.

In *Iron Bravo: Hearts, Minds, and Sergeants in the U.S. Army,* Carsten Stroud describes the reaction of frontline troops to the presence of women. Stroud notes that though an infantry unit poised at the front included no women, trucks carrying supplies and equipment often were driven by women:

> It was weird for the . . . troops to see women so close to the front, but here they were, pushing eighteen-wheelers downrange from the hundred scattered airfields around the desert.

> [Sgt. Dee] Crane found it hard to get used to, seeing girls no older than high school cheerleaders lugging their M16s, wearing Beretta 9-mms slung low like gunfighters, ear-to-ear grins on their faces, adrenalized by the long-haul driving and the war-zone intensity, laughing and flirting with the troopers surrounding them.

gible for activation. Requests for exemptions from the activation would be handled by the military services only on a case-by-case basis. Reserve units need all hands to perform their missions. Except in highly unusual circumstances, they would have them.[32]

Tension between military and family needs came to a head many times, often in the case of single mothers. But overall, single mothers received high marks for their military efficiency. Col. Darrald Hert, an army chaplain during the Gulf War, says single mothers appeared to have greater motivation to excel: "We have more and more competent women in the reserves, especially single mothers. They're not just weekend soldiers. They need the money and they really want to be there and make it work."[33]

Moms in War Zones

For married service couples with children, however, the tension reached a flash point in the cases of two female Pennsylvania reservists, both of whom had husbands already serving in the Gulf. One, who was about to give birth, was given ten days to report or face charges of being absent without leave, or AWOL. The other was in a hospital recuperating from a caesarean section but was given just fifteen days to report for duty. After review, the women were granted six weeks' maternity leave, but the

Being sent to war sometimes created conflicts for single mothers and mothers whose husbands had also been deployed.

initial orders and their individual circumstances spurred a flurry of activity in Congress, where several bills were considered that would have barred the military from sending mothers into war zones.

The legislation irritated many women in the armed services, who believed it would interfere with their ability to make their own family decisions. "Our government trusts us to take responsibility for hundreds of personnel and millions of dollars' worth of equipment, but this legislation is saying we're not capable of making decisions for our own families,"[34] said Lt. Col. Kelly Hamilton, who served for five and one-half months in the Persian Gulf.

Concerns about the deployability of women were also high for those in active service. Although Cheney did not automatically exempt women from service solely because they were mothers, most armed forces did not deploy pregnant women. Because pregnancy essentially disallowed most women from going to the Gulf, some critics charged that servicewomen saw it as a means to get out of what they knew would be unpleasant and hazardous duty. Units typically knew well in advance that they would be deployed to the Gulf, providing women who did not want to go time to try to become pregnant. When at least four of the twenty-two women in the 360th Transportation Company became pregnant prior to deploying to the Gulf, Capt. Steve Fraunfelter, the company commander, said, "I can't say whether they did it on purpose to get out of this, but they knew we were going for more than a month."[35]

The official policy of the U.S. Navy at the time of the Gulf War specified that pregnant women were to fulfill their assignments aboard ship until their twentieth week of pregnancy, at which time the navy's Bureau of Medicine believed "changes in posture and the woman's center of gravity occur which cause problems with balance and decreased agility."[36] But women were routinely sent ashore as soon as it became known they were pregnant, even if they wanted to deploy with their ships. "I got on my hands and knees and begged to stay on board the *Acadia*,"[37] said a personnel clerk who got pregnant while on liberty leave in Dubai. Her fiancé, a boiler repairman on the *Acadia*, completed his tour of duty in the Persian Gulf, but the woman was reassigned to shore duty in the United States.

Mixed Reactions

All told, women were more than three times less likely to deploy to the Persian Gulf with their units than men, mostly because of pregnancy. Moreover, a number of women who did deploy to Saudi Arabia were shipped home early, and pregnancy again was a major cause. Looked at another way, however, less than 0.5 percent of the 23,000 single parents and 5,700 service couples with children were unable to serve in the Gulf War because of family problems. And a study by the General Accounting Office, an investigative arm of Congress, found after the war that single parents had a better Gulf deployment record than bachelors without children.

The reaction of the American public to the deployment of women was mixed, and many were moved by images of soldier-mothers saying good-bye to their children. T. Berry Brazelton, a noted pediatrician, was incensed and offered his opinion that sending mothers to the Gulf was "terrible, reprehensible, and not necessary. . . . A child whose parents leave has two resources. Either to mourn and turn inward or to say, 'I'm bad. Why did my mommy leave me?' Or, 'Is my mommy bad because she left me?'"[38]

A number of women were in fact torn between their military obligations and their devotion to their children. Lori Moore, a former army sergeant, faced that dilemma when her unit was ordered to Saudi Arabia. She sent her three children to live with relatives they had never met, but soon regretted her decision. After further thought, Moore refused to deploy and was discharged from the service: "What I came up with is a mother should be left with her children. I hate to say it because it doesn't fit with the whole scheme of the women's movement but I think we have to reconsider what we're doing." [39]

"They Can't Handle It"

Other women who did deploy developed a new perspective on the idea of women serving in the military. "I don't think females should be over here. They can't handle it. Those feminists back home who say we have a right to fight are not out here sitting in the heat, carrying an M16 and a gas mask, spending sixteen hours on the road every day and sleeping in fear you're gonna get gassed," [40] one woman soldier said.

Once in the Persian Gulf, soldiers could be returned home for up to thirty days of

A female soldier directs aircraft on the ground. After serving in the Gulf War, some women felt that females were less suited to the experience than males.

emergency leave to handle family problems. However, many servicewomen believed they were treated unfairly. Victoria Hudson, who was with the Army Military Police, said women in her battalion were routinely brushed aside in favor of men in requests for emergency leave:

Messages for women from the Red Cross were not acted on. One woman who was married to a Vietnam vet was notified he had had such violent flashbacks watching the war on television that he'd been admitted to a VA hospital on a suicide watch. But her commanders wouldn't let her even call for two weeks. Another woman whose ex-husband had taken her children out of state was so worried she spent a lot of time crying. But instead of getting counseling, she was told she'd have to leave the unit. Still another woman whose children were essentially kidnapped and taken to Puerto Rico was denied emergency leave. But a command sergeant major was given emergency leave because his ex-wife died.[41]

Other women fared better. One woman learned through the Red Cross that her less-than-one-year-old daughter was in the hospital in an oxygen tent. She was granted an emergency leave by her commander, who also happened to have an eleven-month-old daughter. The woman stayed a week with her daughter, then returned to duty.

"He's the Reason I'm Away from My Son"

For many of the women called to serve in the Persian Gulf War, the conflict provided a welcome opportunity to demonstrate that they belonged in the armed forces. Even some mothers believed the sacrifices they were making were essential. Sgt. Deborah Knight, a reservist with the 38th Aerial Port Squadron, was called to serve in Saudi, forcing her to leave her husband and four-year-old son at home. She said she was "scared," but believed she had an obligation to her family to serve. "[Saddam Hussein] right now is the enemy against me. He's the reason I'm here. He's the reason I'm away from my son,"[42] Knight said.

Still other women soldiers believed their presence in the Gulf was nothing short of routine, despite the extraordinary nature of their involvement in a war. Airman 1st Class Kimberly Childress, an air force communications specialist on an A-10 "Warthog" tank-killer squadron, said simply, "It's my job."[43] Lt. Col. Kelly Hamilton, an active-duty pilot in the air force, said, "It's not that people love to go into conflict, but it is rewarding to have your training pay off."[44]

Women serving in the Gulf were deluged by reporters, but generally handled the incessant interview requests with more grace than male soldiers, who considered journalists to be meddlesome pests. Many male soldiers went so far as to nickname reporters PUNTS, or "People of Utterly No Tactical Significance."[45] Photographer F. Lee Corkran recalled one interview of a woman soldier conducted by a reporter from Russia:

> The reporter was interviewing a female Army soldier, and from his questions you could tell he knew very little about the role women play in American society. He asked her if she would rather be home having children. Did she feel out of place wearing Army pants and carrying a rifle? If she came up against a good-looking enemy, would she still shoot him? I might have guessed he was being cynical, but he questioned her with a genuine air of innocence. And the soldier was great. She didn't even blink, just responded with tact and sincerity.[46]

"I Feel Ready"

Maj. Marie T. Rossi of the army's 101st Airborne Division's Screaming Eagles became a potent symbol of women's new role in the military. Prior to the beginning of the ground war, Rossi, who would lead a squadron of Chinook helicopters into Iraq as part of the largest helicopter assault in history, told a CNN interviewer, "Sometimes you have to disassociate how you feel personally about the prospect of going into war and . . . possibly see the death that is going to be out there. But . . . this is the moment that everybody trains for—that I've trained for—so I feel ready to meet the challenge."[47] Rossi later told an ABC reporter, "We thought it was pretty neat that three women were going to be across the border before the rest of the battalion."[48]

The high visibility of women in the Gulf led the press to dub the action the "Mommy War." However, women were specifically barred from serving in combat roles. That did not mean, however, that they were barred from dangerous duty. Sgt. Theresa Lynn Treloar, for example, was given a duty of such great danger she was given the opportunity to refuse. The assignment was so secret that the army would not describe the nature of her duty or allow photographs of her. But Treloar, nicknamed the "Ice Lady" because of her confidence and commitment, said of her assignment, "I chose this and I knew what I was getting myself into when I chose it."[49] Some in the army believed Treloar's secret assignment was so close to the front lines that it violated army policy. But Capt. Michael Mendell, her superior, said, "She is the only woman I know who carries an M-16 rifle, a light antitank weapon, an AT-4 and a grenade. I would trust her to cover my back in any situation."[50]

Hazardous Duty

In some cases, women were in greater danger than their male counterparts, even though they were rarely on the front lines. One of Iraq's most effective weapons during the war was its Scud missiles, which were routinely aimed at rear support positions, where many women soldiers were concentrated. Others were attached to support units assigned to mechanized forces—tank units—and moved into Kuwait and Iraq as

Major Marie T. Rossi led a squadron of Chinook helicopters (pictured) in an assault on Iraq.

the tank units surged forward. Women even served as part of Patriot missile batteries, units that targeted incoming enemy missiles and launched Patriot air-defense missiles designed to blow up the threat.

Women occupied about every job in the armed services except those that involved direct involvement in offensive combat. Deborah Sheehan, a crane operator for a Navy Seabee unit, recalls, "Women served as security, stood guard, manned machine guns. I drove a truck to and from the pier with another woman riding shotgun next to me. We had M-16s, M-60s, and small calibre

hand guns."[51] Women flew and served as crew on planes and helicopters in battle areas, serviced combat jets, launched missiles, and headed support units. Women drove trucks and loaded high-tech bombs on F-117 Stealth fighters. Airman 1st Class Gina Maskunas-Delaney was a crew chief for an F-117, and decided to send the Iraqis a message. On one laser-guided bomb being

Danger in the Rear

Although women demonstrated a higher profile in the armed forces during the Persian Gulf War than at any previous time in history, the military took great pains to keep most women away from duty on the front lines. But isolation from the front was not a guarantee of safety. In *Ground Zero: The Gender Wars in the Military*, Linda Bird Francke notes the difficulty of attempting to keep women soldiers out of harm's way:

> The Army, which sent the most women by far, nearly 31,000, to the Gulf, had long recognized that women faced a high degree of risk on the modern battlefield. Combat scenarios built around a Soviet attack in Europe had always envisioned the targeting of noncombat supply and communication units in the rear. The complicated coding formulas that supposedly kept women out of the most dangerous, frontline combat and combat support jobs would not shield them from the fluidity of the modern battlefield or sophisticated long-range weapons.

Early predictions in the war against Iraq suggested the casualty rate would be higher among the support troops in the rear than in the all-male combat units poised on the border of Kuwait. Not only would the concentration of support troops in the rear make a more productive target for Iraq's maverick Scuds, but it would also be the target of choice for any missile armed with chemical or nerve agents. In the storms and winds of the desert, the commander of the Marine Expeditionary Force reasoned, the nerve gas would be too dangerous for the Iraqis to use near their own frontline troops.

Though Iraq evidently never used its arsenal of chemical and biological weapons, the predictions would become reality. More than half (56 percent) of the 375 U.S. deaths in the Gulf were among noncombat support personnel. According to official casualty records, 15 were women.

Even women who served in the rear in support roles, such as guards (pictured), faced the dangers of battle.

attached to the plane she wrote, "We care enough to send the very best."[52]

Women even served as guards. Sgt. Cynthia Williams was with the Air Force 1st Tactical Fighter Wing Security Police Squadron, and was assigned to guard the gate to an air base in Saudi Arabia. She admitted that periodic Scud attacks were "a jolt" to her, but said she worried more about the possibility of a terrorist attack. But she said she had no qualms about what to do if an attack came: "The gate guards are male and female alike. The women can be shot just like the men. I feel no hesitation in picking up an M-16 and going at it."[53]

"It's Going to Happen"

Lt. Phoebe Jeter commanded an all-male Patriot missile battery. On January 21, 1991, she got her first opportunity to put her training into practice when a Scud attack threatened her base and the Saudi capital of Riyadh. "Everybody was scared . . . we didn't know where they were headed."[54] Within moments, however, Jeter analyzed data about the speed and trajectory of the Scuds, and issued orders to fire. Jeter's unit destroyed at least two Scuds.

Even before the war officially started, the military was braced for the possibility of women casualties but fretted that the American public would react negatively. "But they're going to have to accept it, because it's going to happen,"[55] said 1st Lt. Diana Torres, an operations officer with an ammunition supply unit.

On January 7, 1991, the inevitable happened when Sgt. Tatiana Khaghani Dees, of the 92nd Military Police Company, 93rd Battalion, became the first U.S. servicewoman to die in the Gulf conflict. With her gun pointed at a potential terrorist, she backed off a pier in Dammam and drowned, pulled underwater by the weight of her heavy backpack. Women also died and were injured as a result of traffic accidents. Some of those accidents were the result of blinding sandstorms, but others came about because of sloppy practices. A woman in the military police recounted, "We cleaned up forty bodies in three days that were speed violations. Lives were lost because leaders disregarded directives on safety. There was this feeling that I am God and I can do whatever I want."[56]

Five women lost their lives because of Iraqi fire, including Sgt. Cheryl LaBeau-O'Brien. She was a helicopter technician aboard a Black Hawk helicopter that was shot down over Iraq. Three servicewomen, along with twenty-five servicemen, were killed on February 25, 1991, when a Scud missile destroyed a metal warehouse serving as a barracks in Al Khobar, Saudi Arabia.

POW Threat to National Morale

Major Rossi, thirty-two, who had become a media celebrity when she led a squadron of army helicopters into Iraq at the beginning of the ground war, died along with the three men in her crew on March 1, 1991, a day after the cease-fire. Her Chinook helicopter hit an unlit tower at night.

In addition to possible death of women soldiers, prior to the war military officials also worried about the potential for women to be taken as prisoners by the Iraqis. Nurses had been captured by the Japanese during World War II, and although they had not been mistreated, Pentagon officials were concerned that the capture of a woman soldier would have a negative effect on national morale.

Those fears would be tested in late January 1991 when it was announced that Melissa Rathbun-Nealy, a truck driver with the army's 233rd Transportation Company, had been captured. She was the first enlisted American woman ever to be taken as a prisoner of war. Rathbun-Nealy had been in a truck convoy that became disoriented in the desert. Instead of heading back to their base, as they thought, the soldiers actually found themselves at a battlefield. After discovering their error, the truck drivers attempted to turn around, but the truck Rathbun-Nealy was in was hit by shrapnel and crashed into a wall. Rathbun-Nealy had shrapnel wounds and a bullet in her arm and was taken to a prison cell in Basra and then to Baghdad.

She was released on March 4, 1991, and said she had been treated well: "I'm probably the only POW who gained weight in prison,"[57] she said.

Army flight surgeon Major Rhonda Cornum would endure a more difficult trial after she was taken as a prisoner on February 27, 1991. Cornum was in a Black Hawk search-and-rescue helicopter on a mission to retrieve a wounded air force pilot. After passing over pockets of U.S. and coalition troops, the helicopter came under fire from Iraqis.

Army flight surgeon Major Rhonda Cornum after her release. Cornum was taken prisoner by Iraqi troops after her helicopter came under fire and crashed.

"It was as if we were a lawn mower that had run over a beehive, and the bees were coming up to sting,"[58] she recalled. Then,

> We got hit, then we crashed. . . . After we tumbled and rolled, I found myself underneath at least part of the wreck. I wasn't thinking clearly enough to know why I couldn't use my arms, I used one foot to kind of push my way out from underneath this airplane. By the time I got out, the Iraqi soldiers were there.[59]

"I Wanted to Make It Home"

Both her arms were broken in the crash, a bone in one of her fingers had been shot off, and ligaments in one of her knees had been destroyed. She also was bleeding profusely, the result of a bullet wound in her shoulder. But Cornum was alive, one of three surviving members of the eight-person crew. She and another survivor, Sgt. Troy Dunlap, were thrown over the tailgate of a pickup truck and taken into custody. During her first night of captivity, Cornum was sexually assaulted, but her screams of pain and broken limbs prevented further molestation. "I would have gotten raped but he couldn't get my flight suit off,"[60] Cornum said.

That same flight suit would later prove problematic for Cornum, whose injuries made personal hygiene difficult. Cornum refused an Iraqi offer of surgery that she knew she required, but did permit her guards to remove the suit and provided her with a bathrobe. With her broken limbs, however, she needed assistance with the most personal of matters. Her fellow POWs, and especially Dunlap, gave her the help she needed. "Dunlap was the real star,"[61] Cornum said. "I had my period and they helped me go to the bathroom and remove the tampons and all that stuff. It was bad planning to have my period. I'm not sure what good planning would be, but it just happened that way. I didn't want to die of toxic shock out there. I wanted to make it home."[62]

Women entered the Persian Gulf War weighted with the concerns of military officials and the public about the degree to which they were ready, and willing, to serve in an actual war. Once the shooting began, it became clear that many women were not only ready and willing, but also quite capable of carrying out their duties. Cornum and Rathbun-Nealy met each other for a short time when both were on the *Mercy*, a hospital ship. When asked what it was like to meet each other, Cornum said, "We're both females in the Army. That's about it. Gender doesn't come into play at all, to tell the truth. Nor did it the whole war, which I think is the most important thing you can come away with."[63]

The Thunder in Desert Storm

As ground troops readied for possible battle with Iraq, fighter and bomber pilots also prepared for war. Pilots knew that if Iraq did not leave Kuwait, they would be called on to bomb strategic Iraqi targets, such as communications and radar facilities, so that Iraq would have a difficult time determining American military intentions. In addition, pilots knew they would be asked to bomb bridges and other transportation facilities to make it more difficult for the Iraqi army to maneuver in any ensuing ground war. Some pilots had been training for possible battle with Iraq even before the Iraqi invasion of Kuwait because some military planners thought such a move, if it came, could be a prelude to war.

One group of F-15E "Strike Eagle" pilots at Seymour Johnson Air Force Base in North Carolina had been flying daily missions and were tired, but were up at 3 A.M. readying for their most important mission yet. The goal of the exercise would be to fly into Iraq to demolish four important bridges. By 5 A.M. they were being briefed on everything from the weather conditions surrounding their targets to the terrain to the presence of antiaircraft artillery and surface-to-air missiles—ground-based weapons used to shoot down planes. In addition, the pilots were warned and briefed about Iraqi fighter jets, including the Soviet-made MiG-3 Flogger and the MiG-29 Fulcrum, along with the French-made F-1 Mirage.

First Lt. Robert Del Toro then paused before noting, "And, oh, by the way, I think you should know that in the real world Saddam Hussein just invaded Kuwait. It happened during the night and it looks like he might overrun the country."[64] That early morning announcement on August 2, 1990, was the first news the Strike Eagle pilots had of the Iraqi invasion of Kuwait, a strange coincidence since they were at the end of a training and readiness exercise based on a hypothetical Iraqi invasion. The "Iraqi" targets they were going to "destroy" that day were actually in Virginia.

Training Was Dangerous, But Essential

Once the United States committed itself to a possible war with Iraq, training exercises intensified to ensure pilots were in top form. Pilots flew simulated missions and had mock battles with fighter aircraft in preparation for a possible attack on Iraq.

The training was fraught with danger. In one week in October 1990 alone, four crashes resulted in a number of deaths and injuries. Despite the possibility of death, however, the training missions proved crucial, allowing pilots to learn the best tactics for making their bombing runs and for evading antiaircraft fire.

Training sessions over the vast deserts of the Middle East required some ingenuity because the region was so barren. "When we were on training flights, it was a problem finding a target to practice on out there. Occasionally, we'd go over an oasis, but they weren't like we had them pictured in our minds. Typically, there was just a

Two F-15E "Strike Eagles" streak toward their targets in Iraq.

tank with water and nothing else—no waving palm trees, for sure,"[65] said Capt. Garrett Lacey.

Evening training missions were especially important. Capt. Keith Rosenkranz noted:

Flying at night over sparsely populated areas with no discernible horizon can be difficult, especially in the F-16, with its big bubble canopy. Lights on the ground can easily be mistaken for stars in the sky. What feels straight and level flight could just as easily be a descending left turn. If a pilot becomes disoriented at night or while flying in the weather, he must immediately transition to his instrument gauges and believe what *they're* telling him, not what his senses report. Unfortunately, a lot of pilots think they're infallible when it comes to spatial disorientation. Some will tell you it could never happen to them. But it happens. It happens more often than even the most confident pilots think. Sometimes the results are deadly.[66]

"We Were as Sharp as We Would Ever Be"

The training would more than pay off. Capt. Jay Kreighbaum recalled his first mission of the Gulf War. After penetrating Iraq and evading antiaircraft missiles, Kreighbaum proceeded toward his group's bombing target:

"I Am Truly at Peace"

Prior to the beginning of the air war, pilots had to sort through contradictory feelings about the coming dangers. Some wrote letters to loved ones, knowing that the letters they were writing might be the last loved ones would ever receive. On January 12, 1991, Capt. Keith Rosenkranz wrote to his wife, Colette; his letter is reprinted in *Vipers in the Storm: Diary of a Gulf War Fighter Pilot*.

Hello, my love. I just woke up a few minutes ago and I wanted to share my thoughts and feelings with you. This is a very important letter because we will likely be at war by the time you receive it. I pray that is not the case, but nothing has happened in the last few days to make me think otherwise. . . .

I have no regrets about what I have done or what I am about to do. I would be lying if I told you I wasn't scared. I'm more afraid for you, though, because I know how helpless you must feel right now. The other pilots are just as scared as I am, but if you had to choose a war to fight in, this would be the one. Think back to World War I and II, the Korean War, and even Vietnam. Compare them to the Persian Gulf, and you will realize that America has never held a stronger advantage over its enemy. . . .

I am truly at peace with myself and with God. I'm putting myself in His hands, and I'm doing everything I can to prepare for war. My strength comes from looking at pictures of you and the girls. If you look at mine, it will give you the same strength and love that I feel.

Please don't be upset when you read this letter. Be happy for the love we had -- and more importantly, the love we will have in the future. Have faith that I will return home safely to you. I love you, and I will carry your spirit with me wherever I am.

Love, Keith

We're afraid, of course, but it was just the right amount of fear to give extra alertness without degrading our concentration. At times it seemed like a training flight—we had trained hard for five months and we were as sharp as we would ever be. The mission tasks were automatic and I had to keep reminding myself that we're in Iraq, in Saddam's backyard, and they want us dead—that they would try to kill us.[67]

Prior to the start of hostilities, pilots had to wrestle with their fears and overcome misgivings about taking the lives of others. Captain Rosenkranz remembered conversations he had with his wing chaplain, John W. Pierson. When Rosenkranz first dreamed of flying an F-16, "what I wanted was the challenge of flying the world's best fighter. I never dreamed I would use it for its intended purpose: to kill an enemy and his resources. I was raised a Catholic, served as an altar boy, and attended parochial schools for twelve years."[68]

Rosenkranz's fears and apprehension were far from uncommon. Capt. Rick Henson became particularly concerned as the UN deadline for Iraqi withdrawal from Kuwait approached:

I figured we would lose 25 percent that first night. The threats were tremendous—they had a lot of guns and we assumed that they had all been well trained by the Russians. I think a lot of guys felt that way. I know I owed Chain-

saw [Jim McCullough] thirty dollars because he had sent some flowers to my wife when he went back to Oman. I made it a point to pay him just before the deadline because I figured there was a 1 in 4 chance I might not be coming back.[69]

"I Would Be Wanting to Kill Someone"

Capt. David Castillo believed that U.S. military briefers consistently underestimated the threat posed by Iraq's aging, but determined, air corps: "If someone were trying to bomb my country . . . I would be wanting to kill someone. While we were waiting for that first mission, I just felt that it was going to be a lot uglier than anybody was predicting."[70]

To counteract pilots' fears, military commanders did their best to build the aviators' confidence and prepare them for battle. Prior to the opening assault of the Desert Storm air war, Brig. Gen. Buster Glosson delivered a pep talk to pilots at an air base in Al Minhad, United Arab Emirates.

First he walked the pilots through the international negotiations that had attempted to convince Iraq to leave Kuwait peacefully. Because Iraq had rebuffed those overtures, he then announced,

the greatest air war in military history is about to begin. We are on the verge of decapitating every nuclear, chemical, and biological weapons plant in Iraq.

Iraqi antiaircraft artillery, or AAA, flashes across the sky in Baghdad.

We will crater each and every runway. We will hunt down each and every leader in their country—including Saddam Hussein—and we will eliminate them. We are going to wipe the Republican Guard off the face of the earth.[71]

The pilots cheered, anxious to launch their missions.

"We Expect to Lose Some Brave Men"

Glosson, however, added a strong note of caution: "War is a dangerous business, and we expect to lose some brave men. The first few missions are going to be terrifying. You're going to see more SAMs [surface-to-air missiles] and AAA [antiaircraft artillery] than you ever thought possible. Just remember one thing: Bravery is controlling your fear and apprehensions. Stupidity is having neither of the two.[72] Glosson's manner was reassuring to the pilots, who were completely won over when the general made it clear that the military's goal was to win the war with as few casualties as possible. He told the pilots, "I don't care what anybody says, there is not a single target in Iraq or Kuwait worth losing one American life over. . . . If you roll in on your target, and it doesn't look right, come off, and we'll go back and hit it again the next day."[73]

Glosson's speech had the intended effect. Rosenkranz recalled that following the presentation, "there wasn't a pilot in the room who was not ready to go out and win this war."[74]

American pilots were motivated by pep talks that instilled confidence and emphasized safety.

Preflight Rituals

Preparations for combat missions were highly ritualized. Pilots would don their flight suits and head to a briefing room, where they would be given a packet that included their mission assignment and usually a satellite photo of their target. The briefing that followed was extremely important, as each pilot in the room needed a full understanding of the mission. Once in the air, the pilots likely would not have another opportunity to discuss ground threats or evasive maneuvers.

After assembling, the briefing would begin with a roll call and a synchronization of watches. Pilots were then given a detailed weather briefing, including both current conditions and a forecast for mission time. Pilots also were given an overview of the possible mission hazards from an intelligence officer, as well as special code words the pilots were to use in the event they were shot down. The code words were important because they would be utilized by rescue teams to ensure that a distress call was coming from an American pilot and not an enemy decoy. Other details of the mission, including air-refueling plans and plane spacing, were discussed. Pilots could refuel while in the air by flying beneath large air tankers, from which crewmen would lower a hose to a special receptacle on the planes.

Although training had made the dangerous maneuver almost routine, pilots had to be careful not to collide with the tanker or other planes waiting to refuel. At the end of briefings, pilots also were reminded to pack their gas masks and gas antidote kits.

Following the detailed briefings, pilots would begin flight preparations in earnest. They put on so-called G-suits, which wrap around the pilot's legs and abdomen. The suits have a hose that is plugged into a valve in the cockpit, and when the plane is "pulling Gs," bladders in the G-suits inflate, forcing blood up from the lower extremities. Advanced American combat planes can quickly reach speeds that place nine times the normal weight of gravity on a pilot, and the G-suits, along with breathing and muscle-tightening maneuvers, can keep a pilot from passing out.

Survival Kits

Pilots then put on a survival vest equipped with a variety of items pilots would need in the event they were forced to eject from their planes or were shot down. The survival vests contained a radio, a compass, signaling devices, maps, and first aid kits. Pilots also were given a piece of paper called a "blood chit," with printed messages pilots could hand to civilians if shot down. Emblazoned with an American flag and written in five languages, the blood chit said:

I am an American and do not speak your language. I will not harm you! I bear no malice toward your people. My friend, please provide me food, water, shelter, clothing and necessary medical attention. Also, please provide safe passage to the nearest friendly forces of any country supporting the Americans and their allies. You will be rewarded for assisting me when you present . . . my name to the American authorities.[75]

Some pilots had even more on their minds as they readied for combat. Capt. Merrick Krause, who was known as a careful planner, took planning to an extreme prior to his first mission: "I'm Jewish, and I thought I might have a little more to consider than the other guys when it came to attacking Iraq. I didn't want to take any chances. If I got shot down I did not want to be captured,"[76] he said. Krause was referring to long-simmering hostilities between Arabs and Jews, reflected in the ongoing Middle East conflict between Israel and the Arab world, and the fear that he would be killed if captured by a zealous Muslim.

Krause's fears were not unfounded. Even non-Jewish Americans captured as prisoners of war found themselves suspect in Muslim eyes. Army flight surgeon Rhonda Cornum, who was held briefly as a prisoner of war, remembered the difficulty her male counterparts had in convincing their Iraqi captors that they were not Jewish. Cornum said that the Iraqis "made all the male POWs drop their

"I Am from Attack Squadron 35"

Gulf War pilots risked not only their lives but possible capture as prisoners of war, and feared they would be mistreated by their Iraqi captors.

A number of aviators eventually would find out how unpleasant the experience could be. Acting in complete violation of the Geneva Convention, which sets out rules for the treatment of captured combatants, the Iraqi government displayed captured aviators on television, forced them to make propaganda statements, and threatened to use them as "human shields" by placing them in strategic areas to deter U.S. attacks there.

One of the most widely known episodes of prisoner mistreatment involved the case of U.S. Navy Lt. Jeffrey Zaun. Zaun suffered injuries to his face when he ejected from a damaged plane, and was captured by Iraqis. He was beaten by his captors and forced to make a videotaped statement denouncing the United States. As recounted in *CNN War in the Gulf: From the Invasion of Kuwait to the Day of Victory and Beyond*, by Thomas B. Allen, F. Clifton Berry and Norman Polmar, the taped interrogation of Zaun took place though Zaun had smashed his own nose in an attempt to avoid being forced to make a statement. The interrogation was stilted:

Question: "Would you tell us your rank and name?"

Zaun: "My name is Lieutenant Jeffrey Norton Zaun, United States Navy."

Question: "Your age?"

Zaun: "I am 28."

Question: "Your unit?"

Zaun: "I am from Attack Squadron 35 on the U-S-S *Saratoga* in the Red Sea."

Question: "Your type of aircraft?"

Zaun: "I fly the A-6E Intruder attack aircraft."

Question: "Your mission?"

Zaun: "My mission was to attack H-3 airfield in southwestern Iraq."

Question: "Alone?"

Zaun: "I flew as part of a formation of four aircraft in order to commit this attack."

Question: "What do you think, lieutenant, about this aggression against Iraq?"

Zaun: "I think our leaders and our people have wrongly attacked the peaceful people of Iraq."

Although Iraqi dictator Saddam Hussein intended such displays to sway public opinion against the American-led war effort, it had the opposite effect. President George Bush condemned the forced statements, and Americans continued to support U.S. involvement in the war.

pants so they could see if they were circumcised. These guys had to do a lot of talking to convince the Iraqis that circumcision was an American tradition, not Jewish, or they would have shot them. No question of that."[77]

"This One's for You"

By January 16, pilots were ready to put their training and preparation to the test. Navy weapons specialists aboard ships in the Persian Gulf and the Red Sea were rapidly programming Tomahawk cruise missiles, which stored digital maps of terrain and target images, to guide them to their ultimate destination in Baghdad, Iraq. Meanwhile, in the skies over Saudi Arabia, large refueling planes were topping off the tanks of combat aircraft, and E-3 AWACS, or Airborne Warning and Control System planes, used their radars to keep track of both Iraqi plane traffic and the hundreds of American and coalition aircraft that would take part in the opening strike of the war.

At a Saudi air base, pilots from the U.S. 37th Tactical Fighter Wing readied their F-117A Stealth attack planes for duty, and were soon airborne. By 2 A.M. on January 17, roughly 700 U.S. and coalition planes were in the air, ready to turn Operation Desert Shield, the defense of Saudi Arabia, into Operation Desert Storm, a war to force Iraq out of Kuwait. The well-choreographed effort began when eight AH-64 Apache helicopters from the

army's 101st Airborne Division flew into Iraq to blow up radar stations crucial to Iraq's air defenses. Firing missiles and rockets with names like "Hellfire" and "Hydra," the helicopter assault against the radar installations proved so successful that the large air assault was able to fly into Iraq undetected by radar, meaning that Iraq would have greater difficulty mounting a defense against the planes, which headed for targets deep inside Iraq. In the excitement of bombing the radar stations, one aviator exclaimed, "This one's for you, Saddam."[78]

Then Tomahawk land-attack missiles from the naval cruiser *San Jacinto* and nine warships, including the thundering battleships *Missouri* and *Wisconsin*, were launched,

---

The F-117 Stealth attack plane, designed to evade radar detection, was one type of aircraft used to launch Operation Desert Storm.

and the air war was on in earnest. The gathering storm of fighter aircraft included F-117 Stealth aircraft, specifically made to elude radar detection, and scores of strike aircraft from the air force, navy, and Marine Corps. More than one thousand flights, or sorties, were made by coalition strike aircraft during the first twenty-four hours of the air war, supported by a host of fighter jets, refueling planes, rescue helicopters, and electronic intercept and jamming aircraft. The aircraft bombed strategic targets such as radar installations deep inside Iraq, communications centers and military airfields. The goal of U.S. and coalition military leaders was to both destroy Iraq's intelligence capabilities and prevent Iraqi retaliation. By knocking out radar installations, for example, the Iraqis could not track U.S. and coalition aircraft, while bombing airfields made it nearly impossible for Iraq's air force to get

into the air. By attacking such targets first, military planners believed pilots would face less Iraqi resistance when they later bombed roads, bridges, and weapons factories.

Working Like Pit Crews

During the course of the roughly six-week air war, more than one hundred thousand missions were flown, and the combined explosive power of bombs dropped by coalition aircraft was ten times that of the atomic bomb dropped on Hiroshima at the end of World War II.

Pilots received most of the credit for the success of the air campaign, but a large force of support personnel were necessary to ensure success. As one example, sailors hunched over radar screens deep in the bowels of aircraft carriers served as air traffic controllers, responsible for bringing the navy's jet aircraft to safe landings on five-

"We're Just as Important as the Pilots"

Accolades about the success of the allied air war campaign tended to flow to the pilots and the sophisticated weaponry utilized by pilots during the Persian Gulf War. However, the pilots might not have gotten into the air without a large supporting cast.

A story by *Stars and Stripes* reporter Dave Schad, reprinted in *The Stars and Stripes Desert Storm January 17–February 28, 1991: A Commemorative Edition*, examines the contributions of the often unheralded ground crews. "I think we're just as important as the pilots," Sgt. Tyrone Tillery told the paper. Tillery's commander, Col. Ron Andrea, agreed. "A lot of attention is given to more senior people, but in the mainte-

nance field, there are very few officers or senior enlisted people. A lot of decisions are made by people out on the flight line."

Planes returning from missions would have to be readied for flight in a short time, usually less than an hour. The planes first went into what was called a "hot pit," where they were refueled with roughly 3,800 gallons. The planes also had to be rearmed, and any problems had to be quickly diagnosed and fixed. As Sgt. Bruce Rabie concludes, "The pilots fly them, but the flight-line guys keep the planes working. The pilots are the ones getting shot at and they deserve a lot of credit, but not all of it."

hundred-foot steel runways that pitched and rolled in ocean swells.

Ground crews, too, were pushed to their limits as they serviced, refueled, and rearmed combat planes, especially during periods when planes were under the state of Immediate Combat Turnaround. At such times, planes flying missions made quick stops for fuel, munitions, and sometimes new pilots, and the operations resembled the frenzied activities of pit crews during car races.

Despite the high-tech nature of the weaponry being used by the U.S. soldiers in the air, the arming of planes was decidedly low-tech. Crews cradled missiles in their arms, walked carefully to their planes, and mounted the missiles using nothing more than brute strength and wrenches.

Constant Danger

For pilots and air crews, danger was nearly constant. Capt. Genther Drummond, who took part in the first night of air assaults on Iraq, exulted, "It was as if we had no adversary."[79] But despite the early success of the air warriors, the Iraqis maintained a formidable air defense, including determined crews manning antiaircraft missile batteries, groups of ground-based guns powerful enough to shoot down attacking aircraft. Those guns posed a considerable danger to pilots. Lt. Tyler Kearly described combat missions as "three and a half hours of boredom and ten minutes of stark terror."[80]

Kearly recalled one mission when he found himself being chased by eight sur-face-to-air missiles, which were designed to hone in on hot objects. The heat-seeking missiles could literally follow planes. "I saw a flash on the ground and a cloud of sand. Then I saw a flare go up and I realized it was tracking me. That got my attention. It was pure adrenaline rush,"[81] Kearly said.

First Kill

Some pilots drew particularly dangerous duty, that of protecting bomber planes from Iraqi fighters. On the first night of the air war, Capt. Steve Tate was leading four air force F-15C Eagle fighters from the 71st Tactical Fighting Squadron, 1st Tactical Fighter Wing. The mission for Tate and his fellow pilots was to hunt and destroy Iraqi planes before they could interfere with the missions of other coalition planes.

Well inside Iraq, Tate began to encounter antiaircraft artillery, or triple-A as the pilots called it. Despite the enormous danger the triple-A posed, Tate could not help but be struck by the beauty of the tracers from the artillery fire, which he said resembled "Christmas lights, in all colors."[82] Later, Tate was informed by controllers in a patrolling AWACS that a potential Iraqi plane was nearby. Tate found it, but took time to identify the plane to make sure he would not shoot down an allied plane. He lined it up in his weapon sight and then fired a Sparrow missile, an air-to-air weapon that is guided by radar radiation reflected from the target plane. Tate reported:

There was a large bright flash under my right wing, as the Sparrow dropped off and its motor ignited. . . . It seemed to start slow and then pick up speed really fast. You could see the missile going toward the airplane, and about 2 seconds after [the missile] motor burned out, the airplane blew up.

A huge engulfing fire billowed up. It lit up the sky. You could see pieces of the aircraft in the glare. They burned as they fell.[83]

At 3:15 A.M., Tate had shot down the first enemy plane in the war.

A Carefully Scripted Air War

F-15 pilots like Tate led a demanding life once the air war began. Most flew thirty or more missions, lasting between six and nine hours and requiring three to six aerial refuelings. All pilots knew that any lapse in concentration could lead to their death or the death of a fellow pilot. Tate himself amassed two hundred combat flying hours during the air war, roughly the same amount of flying time an F-15 pilot ordinarily gets in one peacetime year.

Each day of the air war required complicated coordination. Orders were issued every day to assign air routes, times, and altitudes for the hundreds of planes of every service branch of each country in the allied coalition that took part in the air war. Complicating the coordination efforts was the need to keep air corridors clear to accommodate the Tomahawk missiles fired from naval ships in the Persian Gulf and the Red Sea.

To keep track of the extraordinarily complicated air freeways and to ensure that planes did not fly into each other, the military relied on airborne AWACS. Controllers within the planes (which from the outside resemble a jet airliner with a giant rotating radar dome attached to the top) kept track of and managed more than three thousand missions daily—more flights than take off and land daily from Chicago's O'Hare International Airport, the busiest airport in the United States. And yet, there were no aerial collisions. One officer who was responsible for one of the tactical air control centers said the military's air safety record in the Gulf was the result of "training, planning, and an awful lot of luck."[84]

Pilots quickly learned to appreciate the hours of training they underwent prior to the war. Capt. Mike Cloutier recalled a bombing mission against a Scud missile installation at the beginning of the war that required a dive through heavy antiaircraft fire: "This is where training paid off. You do what you have always done, but it is an absolute eternity with all that stuff zipping by the jet and waiting for the bombs to come off."[85]

"It Looks Like a Waterfall"

Although pilots risked their lives every time they took to the air, even during prewar training, in the Gulf War their off-duty lives were often more comfortable than those of ground soldiers. For example, pilots stationed in the United Arab Emirates, where Islamic rules are not as strictly enforced as in Saudi Arabia, were able to enjoy beer when off-duty at a base beer tent. At the air base in Al Minhad, UAE, pilots lived in uncarpeted trailers equipped with a restroom and shower. Though the trailers were rustic, they provided more comfort than a tent in the middle of the Saudi desert.

In the air, however, pilots were rarely comfortable. Many found actual combat even more chilling than their worst imaginings. Maj. Bill Polowitzer was amazed at the amount of antiaircraft fire the Iraqis were able to muster. "It looks like a waterfall, or like a wave or surf over us. We're like inside a black tunnel with the stuff

AWACS (Airborne Warning and Control System) controllers coordinated air traffic, handling over three thousand missions every day.

To lower Iraqis' resistance before the ground assault, B-52s dropped bombs weighing up to two thousand pounds on Iraqi targets.

arcing over our head,"[86] Polowitzer said of the triple-A fire. Capt. Rich Moran, who participated with Polowitzer in a Strike Eagle mission on the first night of the air war, said the antiaircraft fire reminded him of

> the Fourth of July. Suddenly it's the most impressive fireworks display I've seen in my whole life—those I've seen in some of the big cities were nothing in comparison. . . . For a fraction of a second the triple-A looked beautiful, then reality says, these are bullets and only every seventh is a tracer. So we are flying through what must have been almost a solid wall of the stuff and how we were not hit, I do not know. Actually, it was mesmerizing, and it is impossible in words to describe how much there was.[87]

Downed Aviators

By the end of the allied air offensive, coalition forces had flown a combined 109,876 combat and support flights, not counting flights by transport and cargo planes that brought men and supplies to the region. Of those combat missions, 41 coalition planes, including 32 from the United States, were shot down by ground-based guns. In addition, 26 U.S. planes crashed in noncombat accidents. No planes were lost in shootouts with Iraqi fighter jets.

Some pilots and crew members died after being shot down; others were rescued by U.S. search-and-rescue helicopters. A number were captured by the Iraqis and badly mistreated in violation of international agreements designed to protect prisoners of war. Among other things, the Iraqis showed the captured aviators on television, beat them and forced them to make public or taped statements denouncing their actions, and threatened to place them at military installations for use as human shields against allied attack.

Naval aviator Lt. Jeffrey Zaun, a bombardier-navigator, ejected from a damaged A-6E Intruder and parachuted safely along with his pilot, Lt. Robert Wetzel. Zaun decided to stay with Wetzel, who was injured, rather than seek an escape, and was captured by the Iraqis. Zaun was tortured by his captors, and then smashed his own nose in an attempt to avoid being forced to make a propaganda confession on Iraqi television. He was forced to appear anyway, saying, "I think our leaders and our people have wrongly attacked the peaceful people of Iraq."[88]

As the forty-three-day air campaign wound down, the military focused on preparing the way for combat troops and the launch of the ground war. Despite the heavy pounding the Iraqi military had received from allied air attacks, Iraq's army still occupied Kuwait, and ground troops would have to push the army back into Iraq. In an effort to reduce the Iraqis' willingness to fight, much-feared U.S. B-52s bombed Iraqi positions with bombs up to two thousand pounds in size, which had a cheering effect on U.S. troops and were absolutely demoralizing to the Iraqis. The sound of the bombs was like thunder. In addition, air strikes were launched against Iraqi tanks and equipment. Finally, planes dropped propaganda leaflets on Iraqi positions, urging the soldiers to surrender.

"If You Do This, You Will Not Die"

The leaflets promised that any surrendering Iraqis would be treated humanely:

Cease Resistance—Be Safe

To seek refuge safely, the bearer must strictly adhere to the following procedures:

1. Remove the magazine [ammunition] from your weapon.

2. Sling your weapon over your left shoulder, muzzle down.

3. Have both arms raised above your head.

4. Approach the Multi-National Forces' positions slowly, with the lead soldier holding this document above his head.

5. If you do this, you will not die.[89]

From the perspective of U.S. military planners, the air war had been a success. Iraq's radar and communications systems had been destroyed, and by the end of the air campaign U.S. planes controlled Iraqi air space. As a result, U.S. and coalition planes easily could track Iraqi troop movements, while Iraq was unable to monitor the activities of U.S. troops. However, the war over Iraq's invasion of Kuwait was not over. Ultimately, victory would be up to ground troops.

Chapter 5

"If I Don't Get to Kill Somebody Soon . . . "

After months of training and waiting, U.S. ground troops were growing restless and weary. Front-line combat troops huddled in their tents, fighting not an oppressive heat but a relentless rain. Many soldiers had dysentery; others suffered from persistent colds. Some wondered whether after all their training they would sit on the sidelines of the war while Iraq was defeated from the air.

The air war had significantly weakened the Iraqis. Allied air attacks had knocked out Iraqi radar and communications systems, disrupted Iraq's power supply, grounded Iraq's reconnaissance aircraft, and destroyed Iraq's transportation network.

Because of its air superiority, the United States and its coalition allies were able to get a clear picture of Iraqi troops and fortifications. Photo and electronic reconnaissance planes flew over Iraq and Kuwait twenty-four hours a day, giving commanders a bird's-eye view of the sand berms, barbed wire, minefields, and oil trenches Iraq had erected to slow or repel an American attack. Radar planes also flew day and night, providing U.S. commanders with timely information about Iraqi troop movements.

The aerial intelligence was supplemented by the dangerous work of Special Forces teams, which penetrated the borders of Iraq and Kuwait to spy on Iraqi troop movements. Special Forces were small, lightly armed units that had undergone rigorous and intensive training on many aspects of covert, or clandestine, warfare. Their training included practice in making raids, demolition, infiltrating enemy lines, hostage rescue, and reconnaissance. The Special Forces teams worked at night and found cover in the desert during the day. Special Forces also aided bombing runs by aiming laser beams onto military targets; this effort made it easier for laser-guided weapons to reach their targets successfully. The Special Forces teams also played an active role in search-and-rescue missions for pilots shot down in Iraqi territory.

A Feint and a Maneuver

Even prior to the launch of the air war, military leaders saw that Iraqi forces were massed primarily in Kuwait, where they were well entrenched. Gen. Norman Schwarzkopf, the U.S. commander of coalition forces during the Gulf War, worried that a direct attack on the Iraqi positions in Kuwait would produce immense allied casualties and an uncertain outcome, the "mother of all battles" that Saddam Hussein had promised. Even the U.S. Army's AirLand Battle Manual cautions against

frontal attacks on enemy troops: "Envelopment avoids the enemy's front, where his forces are most protected and his fires most easily concentrated. Instead, while fixing the defender's attention forward by supporting or diversionary attacks, the attacker maneuvers his main effort around or over the enemy's defenses to strike at his flanks and rear."[90]

Schwarzkopf decided that, instead of attacking the Iraqi positions in Kuwait from the front, he would move a large mass of troops westward. Those troops—the VII Corps and the XVIII Airborne Corps, more than 250,000 strong—moved more than

Night vision goggles aided soldiers who worked in the dark, such as the Special Forces teams.

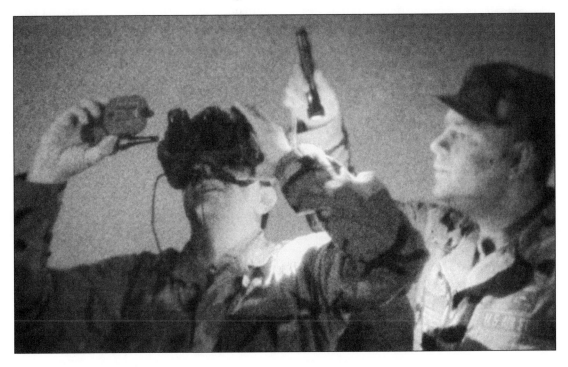

two hundred miles to the west, where they were to attack the more lightly defended southern frontier of Iraq and swing to the east and trap the heavy concentrations of Iraqi troops in Kuwait.

Although difficult in itself, moving the troops was not as difficult as ensuring they were properly supplied. Army logistics experts were strained to the limit. Under original plans, "We would have fourteen days to transport hundreds of thousands of troops, several million tons of supplies, and billions of gallons of fuel, and to set up an effective structure for orderly distribution and resupply,"[91] recalls Lt. Gen. William G. Pagonis. Moreover, the massive effort would require secrecy. Pagonis and his fellow logisticians eventually developed a plan to accomplish the feat in twenty-one days, which was adopted.

A New Logistical Command

Planners set up a new logistical command center in King Khalid Military City in Saudi Arabia, and established a logistics base just outside the city that would serve as a new truck terminal. Code-named Logbase Bravo, the new site was used to load trucks that were sent northward as soon as the air war began. Contents of the trucks would be used to establish two new logistics bases near the border between Saudi Arabia and Iraq.

Two days after the air war began, once it was clear that the Iraqis' ability to see U.S. movements from the air had been eliminated, trucks began streaming across the Saudi desert on their assigned travel routes, transporting troops, tanks, weapons, fuel, and supplies to their new positions along the Saudi-Iraqi border. "During the next month, those roads saw a constant flow of movement—twenty-four hours a day, seven days a week. By the time the pipeline was flowing at full speed, an average of eighteen trucks per minute were crossing through a single point on the northern route. This rate was sustained for an entire month,"[92] Pagonis writes.

By February 3, both the VII Corps and the XVIII Corps were in their assigned attack positions, and by February 20, they were fully equipped with supplies. Supplies continued to flow into the area, however. When the ground war finally began on February 24, the army had put in place enough food and water to last 29 days, enough fuel to last 5.2 days, and enough ammunition to last 45 days. By the time of the cease-fire four days later, as resupply effort continued, there were on hand 29 days' worth of food, 5.6 days' worth of fuel, and more than 65 days' worth of ammunition. The logistics of keeping enough fuel on hand alone were staggering, since the two army corps required close to 4.5 million gallons of gas a day.

"They'll Be There . . . Even Through All That"

Although military leaders had a great deal of faith in the flanking maneuver developed by Schwarzkopf, concerns remained over keeping U.S. casualty figures as low as

possible. Because of the entrenchments and barriers Iraq had constructed to slow an American ground advance, special care was taken prior to the launch of the ground war to bomb the Iraqi fortifications heavily. Fifteen-thousand pound "daisy-cutter" bombs were dropped on Iraqi positions, exploding aboveground and creating shock waves that collapsed Iraqi bunkers. Fuel-air bombs also were used; these weapons, which release a fuel mist that ignites and explodes, killed many Iraqi soldiers in trenches and detonated Iraqi minefields.

As devastating as such attacks were, many U.S. ground troops knew they would

American forces were in their assigned attack positions three weeks prior to the launch of the ground war.

nevertheless face daunting opposition. Sgt. Dee Crane, a veteran of the Vietnam War, openly worried that too much time would elapse between the air bombardment and ground attack. Talking with his captain as U.S. B-52s bombarded an Iraqi position roughly seven miles away, Crane said: "Well, sir, thing is, you can't wait around. We should get in there, hit them as soon as the bombs stop. They'll be dug in and stunned. Our trouble is, we always give them a chance, let them get their balance back. . . . They'll be there, sir. Even through all that."[93]

Although troop morale generally remained high, some soldiers were anxious to make their way into Iraq and bring about an end to the war. Said one soldier, "If I don't get to kill somebody soon, I'm going to kill somebody."[94]

"This Could Be a Long Day"

Commanders did their best to keep the troops confident and focused. Lt. Col. Gregory Fontenot gathered his tank unit around him on the eve of the ground war, telling his men that although their mission would be dangerous, it would be no more perilous than what had been faced by their predecessors in Company C in past wars. Pointing to a map of Iraq he had drawn with chalk on a Bradley fighting vehicle, Fontenot laid out the assignment before them and walked them through the fear he knew was in the heart of every soldier:

> This could be a long day. [But] we aren't some Johnny-come lately . . . outfit. We have a proud record in World War II, we went to Vietnam, and you are the sons and grandsons of the GIs then. You need to live up.
>
> You *will* be afraid. If you're not, there's something wrong with you. You'll know when you're afraid, guys. You'll need to urinate, you'll taste a half-dozen nails, number-ten nails, in your mouth. . . . It's okay to be afraid, guys. Cope with it, deal with it, face it, look at it, examine it,

but do *not* let it dominate you. I'm talkin' no-[kidding], you-believe-you're-gonna-die, afraid. It'll *happen*. The best way to get over it is to fire one round. As soon as you do, you'll know what to do, which is *aim* and *fire* and *advance*. So don't worry.

I don't want to fight fair, guys. I've nothing against the Iraqis, I don't even *know* an Iraqi. For all I know, Rashid and Fatima are a helluva nice couple, the kind you'd have over, but I know this: Rashid and Fatima are wantin' us *dead* and we ain't gonna give 'em their wish. We're gonna—[w]e're gonna *beat* these guys.[95]

At about the same time, a group of soldiers from the 1st Infantry Division visited Sergeant Crane. They had seen aerial pictures of the Iraqi positions they soon would be encountering, and were worried because "it doesn't look to us like there's a lot of damage out there. I mean, things look pretty solid, the berms and [other fortifications],"[96] a soldier told Crane.

"Don't Make Them Bigger than They Are"

Crane took care to build up the soldiers' confidence, while at the same time noting that it would be unrealistic to expect a war without casualties. Still, he said, the Iraqis were probably more scared than the American troops, especially since they experienced heavy sustained bombing: "These guys out there, I guarantee you, they're

The Purpose of Warfare

Some soldiers who witnessed a controversial Gulf War tactic were sickened, but others recognized it as part of the life-and-death struggle that is war. Regardless, most soldiers correctly assumed that publicity would draw public outrage over U.S. conduct of the war.

When American troops rolling through Iraq encountered pockets of stiff resistance from entrenched Iraqi troops, they fired weapons and urged them to surrender. When the Iraqis refused, tanks with bulldozer blades attached to the front simply filled the trenches with dirt, burying the Iraqis alive.

Writing about the tactic in *Iron Bravo: Hearts, Minds, and Sergeants in the U.S. Army,* Carsten Stroud reflects the unsentimental attitude of soldiers:

Let the press get wind of that, they'd be howling like wolves. Maybe that was what came of letting the public wander around with deeply vague ideas about combat, all those John Wayne fantasies about guys only getting shot in polite places, dying neatly in an artful pose against a bamboo plant, looking up with Bambi eyes at their high school buddy—Christ, was there a polite way to kill somebody?

The idea was to kill the enemy. Why was it okay to shoot . . . him, or smash him flat as road kill under a Buff [B-52] strike, or nuke a couple hundred thousand, but for chrissakes don't *bury* them! Civilians.

---

colder and sicker and a damn sight hungrier than you, they got fleas and ticks and dysentery and a lot of them haven't eaten anything but fingernails for weeks. I don't want you to underestimate them, but don't make them bigger than they are."[97]

Crane would soon be proven correct. At 4 A.M. on February 24, the ground war was launched. The navy bombarded Iraqi positions, as did land-based heavy artillery. Then the 1st Marine Expeditionary Force, joined by the army's 2nd Armored Division, punched across the Kuwaiti border, just as the Iraqis had expected. But the move was a diversion, dangerous though the duty was.

At the border between Saudi Arabia and Iraq, the main thrust of the American-led attack was poised for battle. A steady rain of artillery had blasted away at Iraqi positions for an hour, and the air was heavy with the smell of rockets and exploded bombs. When the artillery fire stopped, the troops began to move. The mass of troops and equipment was astounding, including tanks, armored combat earth movers, and Humvees full of infantry and scouts. Helicopters circled overhead. The heavy concentration of raw power gave the troops an exhilarated confidence, and the forces roared into Iraq at speeds of up to fifty miles per hour.

Troops soon encountered Iraqi minefields, but passed through them with little difficulty. Using daisy-cutter bombs and line charges—flexible hoses filled with explosives that were rocketed over a minefield and then detonated—the troops were able to cut a safe swath through the mines. In addition, tanks outfitted with large plows and large metal rollers similar to those used by road crews to smooth asphalt surfaces also were utilized to clear paths through the minefields. The plows then cut holes through the sand berms, and tanks, lightly armored Bradley fighting vehicles, and Humvees full of infantry raced through the breaches.

Some troops traveled on through the night and hardly encountered resistance, but others found themselves under fire from Iraqi soldiers. In the fight bombs, sand, and stones filled the air, as bullets flew in all directions. Apache helicopters joined the fray, firing at Iraqi tanks to the rear of trenches filled with firing Iraqi soldiers.

Surrender

Virtually within hours, Iraqi return fire diminished, and many Iraqi troops fled the trenches, waving white cloths to surrender. One soldier recalled, "A lot of those Iraqis on the front line were just waiting for us to get there. They were stuck out there. They had minefields in the front of them, and

The ground troops advanced from Saudi Arabia into Iraq at speeds of up to fifty miles per hour.

tanks or Republican Guards behind them, so they couldn't go anywhere. They just had to wait until we got there so they could surrender."[98]

Some soldiers were moved to tears by the ragged state of the surrendering Iraqis, most of whom wanted nothing more than something to eat. Soldiers threw packages of MREs to them as they were waved to the rear, and some of the Iraqis were so hungry they fought among themselves for the food packets.

One unit that rolled into Iraq initially met only token resistance, and was soon swarmed by Iraqi soldiers hoping to surrender. While most communication between the enemy warriors was difficult because of language differences, there were moments of humor. Second Lt. David J. Russell used unsophisticated English to interrogate an Iraqi prisoner. Pointing to his own tank, Russell said, "Tank. You know tank? Is tank. Iraqis have tank?" The Iraqi answered, "Yes. But your English isn't very good."[99]

"It Is Huge"

Because of reports that surrendering Iraqis might actually be troops on suicide missions laden with explosives that would detonate in the midst of U.S. forces, the Iraqis were lined up and ordered to strip to their underwear when taken into custody. One Iraqi began to cry as U.S. soldiers yelled at him to undress. Sergeant Crane intervened, realizing the man had been so scared he had emptied his bowels. Addressing one of the U.S. soldiers who had been yelling at the Iraqi, Crane said:

You're gonna find, in this pack alone, a whole bunch of them will have done that. They can't help it. It happens to everybody if it gets bad enough. You never been shelled, or got your berm pounded by a [B-52]. It's an automatic response, you can't help it. Only way to get around it, hit the latrines every chance you get, so when it gets hairy, you're empty. Getting shelled, it's the worst. It's like, you lie there, you're more scared than you ever been, only you can't *do* anything about it. That's worse than a firefight, because in a fight, you can change the situation, but when you're on the wrong end of [artillery], each round comes in, it goes through you like a jolt of electricity, or like you were lying under a subway train. It is *huge*. These guys, they've been to a place I hope you never go.[100]

The warfare became particularly ugly when soldiers in the field had to make value judgments weighing U.S. lives against Iraqi lives. As American troops made their way through Iraq, waving surrendering soldiers to the rear, they focused their attention on pockets of resistance from Iraqi infantry. Behind the trenches, Iraqi tanks and artillery burned and smoldered. The U.S. tanks and earth movers outfitted with the big plows cut through razor wire and made their way to positions along the

Overpowered by the ground assault, some Iraqi troops surrendered (pictured), but others kept up the fight.

trenches that continued to fire on the American troops. Loudspeakers broadcast a message urging the troops to surrender, but still some Iraqis continued to fire. The earth movers, with plows down, then slowly rolled down the trenches, filling them in as tanks fired into the trenches. The Iraqi resisters had been buried alive.

Soldiers who witnessed the scene were shocked. Sgt. Achmed Shabazz muttered something as he made his way back to his infantry fighting vehicle following the live burial, attracting the attention of Sergeant Crane. Crane asked Shabazz what he had said. Shabazz answered that he had uttered a prayer. When Crane asked Shabazz for

whom he had prayed, Shabazz said with resignation, "Man, I don't know."[101]

"I'm Running Over This Guy"

In other situations, tanks simply ran over enemy troops, a brutal tactic used to avoid the risk of enemy fire on American troops. Company C faced this problem not long after it rolled into Iraq:

The driver of [Capt. Robert A.] Burns's tank gasped, and the gunner said,

"*Hey!* There's a guy there!" and put his fingers on his red triggers, waiting for Burns's command of "Fire!" But fate was frowning tonight, for C was going southeast and a half-mile past the Iraqi was Company B, the ultimate destination of any hot bullets from C, and Burns addressed his driver, not gunner, and said, "Run him over. . . ."

"I'm running *over* this guy!" Burns radioed to C. . . . The tank seemed to hit a speed bump, the treads presumably turned the man to a bag of white pebbles, white gravel, the tank rolled on. "You got him," said Burns. "How do you feel about it?"

"It was awesome," said [Specialist Samuel T.] Anderson. . . .

"You shouldn't feel that way," said Burns.

"Sir?" said Anderson, not understanding.

"You're killing a guy with a 60-ton tank."

"Okay," not wanting to argue with him.

"I feel [terrible]," said Burns.[102]

Soldiers would never forget their first glimpse of enemy dead. After the initial battles in Iraq, troops moved past the Iraqi fortifications and saw blackened bodies that had been burned by explosions, heaps of mangled bodies hit by missiles, and bodies shredded by machine-gun fire. They saw heads that had no faces, intestines, and internal organs. The battlefield was stained with blood, and a sickening stench filled the air. It was a sobering experience for the troops, who understood that those dead bodies could just as easily have been their own.

The technology available to U.S. troops in the field was the most advanced ever used in warfare, and gave them a huge advantage over the Iraqis. The U.S.-led coalition troops, for example, had handheld electronic compasses linked to global positioning satellites, and night-vision goggles and other devices

Many soldiers were shocked at their first sight of Iraqi bodies.

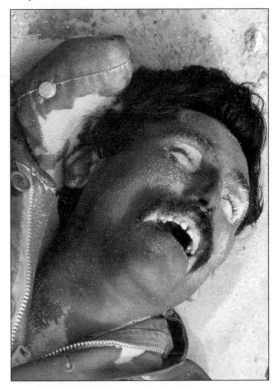

73

that allowed them to see the Iraqis well before the Iraqis could see them. Moreover, the U.S. tanks—the M1A1 Abrams—had greater range than the Iraqi tanks, and highly accurate computer-assisted firing mechanisms. The tanks were even equipped with fax machines and modems, and it was not unusual for commanders to use laptop computers in the field.

Confusion of Battle and Friendly Fire

Despite the advanced technology available, tank battles could be incredibly confusing for troops. At night from great distance, some had difficulty determining whether an armored vehicle to their front was a friendly Bradley or an enemy tank. As a result, some leaders became exceptionally cautious. They believed the U.S. troops, armed with high-power weapons that could kill even at great distances, posed almost a greater danger to themselves than the Iraqi enemy. They feared they could kill U.S. troops with "friendly fire" if they did not make sure their targets were Iraqi tanks.

Those fears proved well founded. Many American casualties in both the air and ground war, which totalled 144 killed in action and 399 wounded in action, were the result of friendly fire. Even unexploded bomblets dropped from U.S. planes, which soldiers called Easter eggs, posed a large threat. Despite orders not to touch the bomblets, a number of soldiers thought the bomblets were duds and picked them up as war souvenirs, a lethal mistake as a number

of the bomblets later exploded when handled.

Although unexploded bomblets were sometimes lethal, the greatest danger to troops outside of Iraqi fire was so-called friendly fire, which occurred when U.S. troops were mistaken for Iraqis and shot at by fellow American troops. Sgt. Ken Kozakiewicz was one of several soldiers standing around a Bradley fighting vehicle that had received a direct hit. The soldiers were angry because they had been hit by a U.S. tank. Kozakiewicz was later photographed as he was rushed by helicopter from the scene with a broken hand when he learned that his friend, the driver of the Bradley, had been killed. The obvious pain in Kozakiewicz's face made the photo one of the most gripping of the war, but that incident was hardly the only case of deadly friendly fire. Four U.S. servicemen lost their lives during the first hours of the war when their Bradley was blown up by a tank crew that believed they had engaged an Iraqi unit.

The Elite Republican Guard

But soldiers in tanks knew that too much caution was dangerous. They feared that by the time they were allowed to shoot they would be under enemy fire. Other commanders, however, were more aggressive, and urged their troops to fire whenever they got a chance. Tank gunners and loaders in these outfits listened to heavy metal rock music on their personal cassette players as they fired at will at Iraqi targets.

After rolling through Iraq, troops received orders to head east to engage the vaunted Tawakalna Division of the Republican Guard, which was positioned in the northern Kuwaiti desert. The Republican Guard was Saddam Hussein's elite force, made up of specially trained soldiers, many of whom were battle-hardened veterans of Iraq's eight-year war with Iran. Within two hours, the battle began when U.S. forces came upon a group of Soviet-made T-72 tanks, one of the hallmarks of the Republican Guard troops.

Pvt. Frank Brandish was in one of the first Bradleys to encounter the Iraqi tanks, and the Bradley was hit before anyone aboard it could launch an antitank weapon. Brandish emerged from the wrecked Bradley as soldiers on another Bradley blew the tank up with a missile. Two of the crew on Brandish's vehicle were dead, but Brandish crawled back in after a couple of wounded survivors. He located a flare to alert medics to his position, but had to pull the cap of the flare off with his teeth because three of his fingers had been blown away in the tank strike. When medics finally arrived, Brandish was back in the Bradley, trying to remove ammunition from the vehicle so it would not explode and kill more of his comrades. Brandish's commander, Lt. Col. John Kalb, said, "They had to pull him out of there. Only then did he look down and notice that he was covered with blood."[103]

"He Bit Off More than He Could Chew"

The noise of battle was near deafening for the troops. Artillery guns rumbled, and the M1A1 Abrams tanks began firing on the

---

A War of Words

On February 23, 1991, President George Bush announced that the long-awaited ground war had begun. Bush accused Iraqi dictator Saddam Hussein of destroying Kuwait instead of withdrawing from the country.

As reported by the Associated Press and reprinted in *The Stars and Stripes Desert Storm January 17–February 28, 1991*, Bush declared:

> The liberation of Kuwait has now entered a final phase. I have complete confidence in the ability of the coalition forces swiftly and decisively to accomplish their mission.

> Tonight, as this coalition of countries seeks to do that which is right and just, I ask only that all of you stop what you were doing and say a prayer for all the coalition forces, and especially for our men and women in uniform, who this very moment are risking their lives for their country and for all of us.

Saddam Hussein also invoked God in announcing the allied ground offensive to the Iraqi people. As reprinted in *The Stars and Stripes*, he said:

> Fight them, oh brave, splendid men. Oh men of the mother of battles. . . .

> Fight them with your faith in God. Fight them in defense of every free and honorable woman and every innocent child, and in defense of the values of manhood, values and the military honor which you shoulder. . . .

> Fight them and show no mercy toward them, for this is how God wishes the faithful to fight the infidel.

Iraqi tanks. The T-72 crews fired back, and from the rear the army utilized multiple-launch rocket systems against the Iraqi tanks. A-10 Thunderbolt aircraft, nick-named Warthogs by pilots and soldiers, circled the battlefield, taking turns making passes at Iraqi tanks, firing spent-uranium-tipped bullets at the tanks.

Soaking it all in, Sgt. Richard Cox sat with the rest of the Army's baggage [support] column as Apache helicopter gunships hovered above. Cox said Iraqi leader Saddam Hussein "asked for it. He bit off more than he could chew."[104] Soldiers' radios crackled with orders and warnings. Col. William Nash, commander of the 1st Brigade of the army's 3rd Armored Division, checked with all his units to make sure they were out of harm's way before calling in an air attack on a column of Iraqi tanks. A junior officer interrupted Nash, urging him to use ground forces instead of

an air attack. "Get a company in there and shoot 'em up. Give them a chance to die!"[105] the junior officer said. But Nash stuck with an air attack, giving the go-ahead to one of the hovering Apaches, which was code-named Death Dealer. "Roger. You may kill them,"[106] Nash told soldiers in the Apache.

As the battle wore on, it became difficult for commanders to call in air power because U.S. troops were in such close proximity to the Iraqis. Soldiers were engulfed in a confusing firefight. Sgt. Glen Wilson, a gunner on an Abrams, found himself surrounded by T-72s. The driver warned of a tank on one side, while the ammunition loader warned of a tank on the other. "It was real confusing,"[107] Wilson said, but his choices became easier when

A-10 Thunderbolts, or Warthogs, fired on Iraqi tanks as the ground battle raged below.

he found an Iraqi tank directly in front of him. Wilson fired and blew up the tank, one of five he would destroy.

"You Basically Didn't Sleep"

The army's baggage column strained to keep up with the advancing U.S. troops. Sergeant Cox directed vehicles through small openings that had been cleared through minefields, pathways that were marked by the green glow of chemlights, similar to the glow-in-the-dark necklaces popular with children. Those that did not stay in the path faced danger. One driver ran over a mine, but was fortunate. All four of his tires were destroyed, but he was alive.

As the soldiers raced through Iraq and Kuwait, they had little time for rest. Breaks lasted as little as a few minutes, and at most a couple of hours. Some hung hammocks in their tanks, and others slept sitting up. Support troops also endured hardships as they tried to keep the combat troops fully supplied. Army handbooks state that a mechanized division will use about 1 million gallons of fuel a day when on the move. But the 24th Infantry Division alone consumed around 2 million gallons of fuel a day. "For those few days of the ground war, it was real hard," recalls then-Sgt. Bill Touchette, who volunteered to drive fuel to front line troops. "You basically didn't sleep."[108]

Prior to the start of the ground war, most American troops had never experienced battle. As they trained and waited, many grew anxious for their role in the conflict to begin. Once they experienced combat, however, most troops felt sympathy for their adversaries and hoped for a quick end to the war. Because of the vast technological advantage enjoyed by the Americans, the war would end quickly. But just as air power alone could not defeat Iraq, ground troops were aided in their efforts by the sea-based navy.

"The Air Force Can't Do Everything"

Although combat pilots and ground soldiers received most of the attention in media coverage of the Persian Gulf War, the U.S. Navy also played a significant, if often overlooked, role in the conflict. U.S. sailors, however, felt separated in large part from the war. "You look outside and you just see water, you don't see bombs going off or dead bodies,"[109] said Janice Evans, an operations specialist on the *Niagara*, a naval supply ship. Although the U.S. Navy did not face a significant naval threat, its presence in the Gulf was crucial to allied missions.

In the tense days after Saddam Hussein's invasion of Kuwait, sailors were given responsibility for enforcing a UN trade embargo against Iraq. Sailors also had to prepare for the possibility of war.

Military leaders were especially concerned that after annexing Kuwait, Iraq would storm Saudi Arabia. However, it would take time for U.S. air and ground forces to arrive and form a defensive force, and responsibility for preventing further Iraqi incursions fell to the U.S. Navy. A number of American warships were in the Gulf region already, as the United States had decided as early as 1949 that political instability and conflict in the Persian Gulf region could greatly affect life in the United States, and regularly deployed forces on maneuvers there. But the greatest military need at the time of the invasion of Kuwait was for aircraft carriers, and the nearest vessels of that class were the *Independence*, in the Indian Ocean at the time, and the *Dwight D. Eisenhower*, in port, in Naples, Italy.

A Crucial Role

Carriers, informally known as flat tops, were critically needed in the Gulf because their combat planes would be crucial to the early defense of Saudi Arabia in the event of an Iraqi attack. Most aircraft carriers had 85 planes, including F-14A Tomcat fighter jets, F/A-18 Hornet striker-fighters, dual-

The aircraft carrier USS Independence *arrived in the Persian Gulf on August 7, 1990.*

mission aircraft, and A6E Intruder attack planes. Flat tops also carried planes designed to attack enemy submarines, planes with sophisticated radar surveillance equipment that could monitor enemy movements, and planes that carried equipment used to jam the electronics of enemy planes.

The crew of the *Independence* rushed the carrier to the Gulf region on August 7, 1990, the same day the *Eisenhower* sailed through the Suez Canal. Meanwhile, the *Saratoga*, another aircraft carrier, set sail for the Middle East from the United States. By war's end, six carriers were in the Gulf region.

The navy's carrier planes were supplemented with ground-based patrol and surveillance aircraft. Navy Seahawk combat-rescue helicopters helped fill out the navy complement. Along with air force Pave Hawk choppers, the Seahawks flew dangerous rescue operations, including flights deep into Iraq, to save downed fliers.

Marine Corps aircraft, both on board navy ships and ground based, also took part in the war. Marine helicopters and AV-8B Harrier jump-jets, so called because they can take off and land vertically, flew missions over Kuwait from navy helicopter carriers in the Gulf.

An F-14A Tomcat fighter jet, one type of aircraft brought to the Gulf, is catapulted from the deck of an aircraft carrier.

Once in the Gulf, seamen immediately became involved in enforcing the embargo against Iraq. UN Resolutions 661 and 665 allowed U.S. and coalition ships "to halt all inward and outward maritime shipping in order to inspect and verify their cargoes and destinations."[110] The embargo prohibited the shipment of war matériel into Iraq, and banned the export of oil from Iraq. Because of the possibility that banned cargo could be routed to Iraq through third-party ports, naval scrutiny entailed extra vigilance. Naval enforcement of the embargo is estimated to have cost Iraq $30 million a day in confiscated goods and lost trade.

A Sometimes Tricky Job

Sailors from the American missile cruiser *Biddle* were the first to board an Iraqi ship under the embargo. On August 31, 1990, they stopped and boarded an Iraqi tanker, which was found to be empty and allowed to continue to Jordan. U.S. Navy and coalition naval vessels intercepted an average of forty ships a day and boarded roughly four a day. By the middle of January 1991, 6,960 ships had been intercepted, and 832 turned away from the Gulf because they carried cargo prohibited under the trade embargo. At times, the work was routine, but sailors had to be ready for anything. On December 26, 1990, an Iraqi freighter refused to stop and tried to keep inspectors from boarding. The ship finally stopped after navy ships fired warning shots. The ship was found to be carrying cargo banned by the embargo

The First Casualty

On Jan. 19, 1991, the Pentagon announced that Navy pilot Lt. Cmdr. Michael S. Speicher was the first casualty of Operation Desert Storm. Speicher, a 33-year-old from Jacksonville, Florida, was listed as missing in action when his F/A-18 Hornet was shot down by an Iraqi surface-to-air missile on the first night of the air war.

and was turned away. Another ship refused to allow an inspection even after warning shots were fired and navy combat planes flew low over the ship. Eventually, two marine helicopters forced the ship to stop, and after an inspection was allowed to proceed.

As soon as aircraft carriers entered the Gulf region, naval aviators began flying reconnaissance missions. The flights both helped in enforcing the embargo and in providing intelligence information about Iraqi troop movements. The rapid naval deployments represented the opening salvo of Operation Desert Shield.

Hospitals Laid the Groundwork for War

Manning the ships of the Gulf War were sailors much younger than their ground soldier counterparts. The average age of sailors serving in the Gulf was under twenty years; the average soldier was twenty-seven.

One of the navy's biggest contributions prior to the war was the establishment of hospital facilities. Navy Seabees, or engineering units, built hospitals, which both ensured the military would be ready to treat injured soldiers and sent a clear signal to Saddam Hussein that the United States was bracing for a war. The navy's Fleet Hospital Program further expanded medical care facilities for those serving in the Gulf. Each facility was designed to provide medical and dental services to as many as five hundred patients and could operate for about a month without being resupplied.

Naval reservists played a large role in staffing the navy hospitals. Then-Assistant Secretary of Defense for Reserve Affairs Stephen M. Duncan writes that much of the work would not have been possible without the reserves:

Ultimately, over 10,000 reserve medical personnel were called up for Desert Storm, half of all the naval reservists activated. Fortunately, the operational success of U.S. forces and the president's policy decision to minimize casualties rather than to force the earliest possible ejection of Iraqi forces from Kuwait prevented a full test of the capabilities of the many medical units of all the services in the theater. Naval reservists had, however, formed an important part of

The navy set up extensive medical care facilities and called up over 10,000 reservists to staff them.

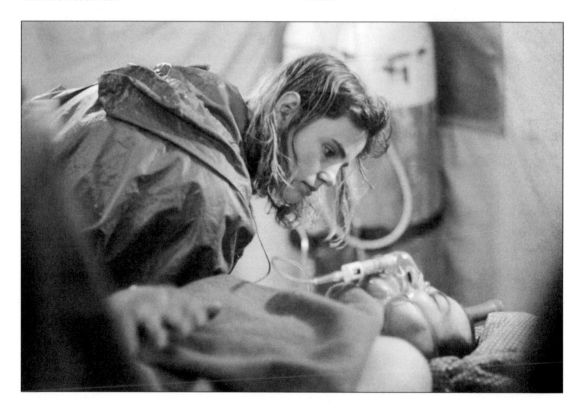

the largest and best medical force deployed to the Middle East since World War II. They had deployed to one of the harshest environments in the world even as they simultaneously helped maintain all other worldwide navy medical care commitments. Even though they were ready for much more tragic circumstances, Naval Reserve medical personnel ultimately spent far more of their active service treating dehydration, minor injuries, and routine medical problems than life-threatening battle wounds. Not one American combatant complained.[111]

The navy's medical contributions were significant, and bolstered the U.S. war effort enormously. During the course of the Gulf War, doctors, nurses, pharmacists, and other naval personnel aboard the *Mercy* and *Comfort* treated thousands of soldiers, most often for noncombat injuries such as dehydration. The first person to be awarded a Purple Heart in the Persian Gulf War was a navy medic. The Purple Heart is the American military medal awarded to personnel

The USS Missouri, *one of two battleships in the Gulf. The* Missouri *could fire two-thousand-pound shells at targets twenty miles away.*

wounded or killed in action. Corpsman Clerence D. Conner was hit by shrapnel from enemy fire while on a marine patrol near the Kuwaiti border. Marine Brig. Gen. Thomas V. Draude said of Conner, "I'm damned proud of him. We were standing by his bedside and he said, 'Please, don't send me home. I've got to get back to my unit. They're depending on me.'"[112]

"There Goes Another Beetle"

By the time Operation Desert Storm was launched, the navy had orchestrated its largest buildup since World War II, amassing more than one hundred ships in the region, including the battleships *Missouri* and *Wisconsin*. The massive ships, the only operational battleships in the world, bristled with nine 16-inch guns. A photographer watching the *Missouri* fire its big guns was awed by the spectacle: "Some said the USS *Missouri* fired a shell the weight of a Cadillac, but most agreed it was closer to a VW. One first saw a flame-burst, then heard a roaring boom, at which time someone always remarked, 'There goes another Beetle.'"[113] The battleships shot two-thousand-pound high-explosive bombs and were highly accurate at distances of more than twenty miles.

Capt. David Bill, commander of the *Wisconsin*, said the nearly fifty-year-old ships were as useful as ever: "There's a lot of years left in these old gals. They may be old chronologically, but they're really teenagers, and they're still ready to go to work."[114] However, the dreadnoughts were costly to oper-

ate, each requiring sixteen hundred crew members, and were showcased in the Gulf primarily as a symbol of brute force.

Their presence was not merely symbolic, however. The *Missouri* and *Wisconsin* fired nearly nine hundred rounds from their guns during the war. Although their accomplishments were often overlooked because of the phenomenal success of the allied air offensive, the battleships undertook important missions. "This is really and truly an Air Force effort . . . and we're participating and we're trying to add to it as best we can,"[115] said Rear Adm. Douglas J. Katz. The crew of the *Missouri* found a way to help when it fired seven shells from its massive guns, destroying an Iraqi command center near the Saudi border. "We have done our job of clearing the coastline and now we are going to move in close,"[116] said Cmdr. Mark Lawrence, an intelligence officer aboard the nuclear-powered carrier *Roosevelt*. Added Lt. Bill Harrop, "The Air Force can't do everything."[117]

Attacks by the battleships drew Iraqi ire, and fire. Iraqi forces attempted to sink the *Missouri* with a Chinese-made Silkworm missile, but navy surveillance aircraft spotted the missile and a British destroyer hit it with missiles before it reached the battleship. Despite their contributions, the battleships would be retired at the end of the Gulf War.

Navy Wears Many Hats

As Desert Shield stretched out, and air force units and ground troops continued to flood

Dangerous Waters

Although Iraq's navy was relatively miniscule to begin with, the U.S. Navy all but obliterated it shortly after hostilities commenced in the Persian Gulf War. However, Iraq continued to pose a threat at sea, dumping explosive mines in waters throughout the Persian Gulf region in a bid to sink or damage U.S. ships. The Iraqi mines were designed to explode when triggered by either the sound, water pressure, or magnetic attraction of a passing ship.

On February 18, 1991, two U.S. warships struck mines. Seven crew members were injured in the blasts, but both ships—the Tripoli, a minesweeper, and the Princeton, a high-tech missile cruiser—remained under their own steam and neither was in danger of sinking.

The navy destroyed nearly a hundred Iraqi mines during the Persian Gulf crisis.

The USS Tripoli *is inspected in drydock after striking an Iraqi mine.*

into Saudi Arabia, sailors played a large role in war preparations. In addition to enforcing the trade embargo against Iraq, sailors searched for mines that were laid in Gulf waters at night by Iraqi ships. Sailors on small wood- or fiberglass-hulled ships were constantly on the lookout for mines, and naval crews in Sea Dragon helicopters from the *Tripoli* towed devices designed to detonate mines through Gulf waters. The *Tripoli* itself was damaged by a mine on February 18, as was a navy cruiser. Those were the only ships to be struck by mines during the conflict.

Naval amphibious ships carrying U.S. Marines and their equipment cruised the Gulf. By the time Desert Storm was under way, roughly ninety-three thousand marines were in the Gulf region, many aboard ships steaming in the Gulf. When not in training missions, the marines continued to work to stay in shape, often doing pushups on ship decks. Marine Corps commandant A. M. Gray said, "There are four kinds of marines: those in Saudi Arabia, those going to Saudi Arabia, those who want to go to Saudi Arabia, and those who don't want to go to Saudi Arabia but are going anyway."[118]

Naval and marine forces carried out a number of training missions during Desert Shield, operations known by such ominous-sounding code names as Imminent Thunder. Marines on amphibious naval vessels practiced landing on the Oman and Saudi coasts, while navy pilots from the three aircraft carriers in the Gulf region took to the air to practice supporting maneuvers and battleship crews perfected bombing techniques.

A Tomahawk Chop

Just as the navy helped launch Desert Shield, it also helped usher in Desert Storm. U.S. Navy technicians aboard missile ships spent the day of January 16, 1991, entering target information into Tomahawk missiles. Originally developed to deliver nuclear weapons, the Tomahawk proved to be an effective weapon during the Gulf War.

A destroyer launches a Tomahawk, a missile capable of carrying a 1,000-pound warhead up to 700 miles.

The non-nuclear Tomahawks used in the Gulf War were similar to airplanes, but they were piloted by computers instead of people. Using altitude-sensing radar to navigate their way to targets, the Tomahawks' computer "pilots" compared the terrain below them in flight against maps that had been programmed into their memory. Vice Adm. Stanley Arthur said the Tomahawks were invaluable because they could be launched even in inclement weather: "During periods of bad weather when you needed to keep the pressure on Baghdad, you could continue to keep their eyes . . . open."[119] Tomahawks could travel up to 700 miles, and their 1,000-pound warheads were capable of penetrating reinforced concrete bunkers. A total of 16 U.S. Navy surface ships and two nuclear submarines launched Tomahawks during the war. Desert Shield became Desert Storm when the *Missouri* and *Wisconsin* launched the first of 52 Tomahawk missiles toward targets in Iraq.

Another navy missile utilized during the Gulf War was the so-called SLAM, or Stand-off Land Attack Missile. With a range of around 70 miles, the missiles are guided to targets by signals from Global Positioning System satellites. As a SLAM nears its target, an infrared camera aboard the missile activates, sending a picture to personnel on a controlling aircraft. The technicians can then guide the missiles into their targets. Two SLAM missiles fired from an aircraft carrier in the Red Sea destroyed an Iraqi power plant. The first bored a hole in the facility, and the second steered through the hole and exploded inside the plant.

Weapons such as the Tomahawk and SLAM provided the United States with an immense advantage during the conflict. Because they could be used against rela-tively small targets with a high degree of accuracy and could be fired from great distances, American forces could use the weapons without jeopardizing the lives of the attacking sailors.

Pioneers in the Skies

Another lifesaving device was the unmanned, Israeli-developed Pioneer. Pioneers resembled small airplanes and were used for reconnaissance and to identify possible bombing targets. The Pioneers carried television cameras that could relay pictures to sailors manning battleship fire control panels, who in turn could fire on the targets. The drones also kept sailors aware of potential Iraqi threats. One captured images of Iraqi boats that were believed to have been carrying Iraqi intelligence officials. The boats were destroyed by navy attack planes. A Pioneer launched from the *Missouri* even "captured" hundreds of Iraqi soldiers, who surrendered to the radio-controlled craft after heavy bombing. The Pioneers were retrieved after missions when radio controllers guided them into large nets stretched across ship decks.

As Desert Storm erupted late on January 16, U.S. aircraft carriers began catapulting planes that undertook a variety of missions, including air strikes and combat air patrols deep within Iraq. From then until the end of the Gulf War, carrier flight operations were nearly constant. Navy and marine pilots flew more than 216,000 combat and support missions, including attacks on Iraqi naval ships that tried to escape to

Iran. The planes destroyed all but one of the roughly twenty ships that attempted to flee the war. The nearly constant carrier flight operations put a strain on flight deck crewmen, who did everything from placing bombs on planes and readying them for launch to securing planes to carrier decks with heavy chains.

Navy pilots also were significantly aided in their missions by on-ship air controllers, who worked in dark rooms below deck sitting in front of banks of radar and computer screens. The controllers, who managed naval air traffic and cleared pilots for takeoffs and landings, were responsible for getting the planes safely back on ship.

"We Couldn't Take the Risk"

Naval aviators, like their air force colleagues, went through extensive briefings prior to their missions. The pilots received an information packet for every mission they flew. Among other things, the packets included descriptions and pictures of their targets, flight routes and altitudes, attack time windows, and identification codes the pilots would need to know in the event they were forced down and called for rescue. The identification codes came in handy for one pilot shot down while participating in a bombing run in Iraq. Two air force A-10 jets, known as Warthogs, and a search-and-rescue helicopter got a radio plea for help from the pilot, and after confirming that the distress call was legitimate, headed off to pick the pilot up. As the aircraft neared the area, they saw an Iraqi truck headed toward the downed aviator. The Warthogs strafed the truck with heavy machine-gun fire, setting it ablaze. The helicopter then dropped down for the rescue. Capt. Randy Goff, one of the Warthog pilots, said they had no choice but to shoot the truck: "We could not allow him [the truck] to be there. We couldn't take the risk."[120]

Naval forces often undertook missions that required coordination with other service branches. For example, army helicopters took off from the *Nicholas* to attack offshore oil platforms occupied by Iraqis. Naval gunfire complemented the successful assault, which resulted in the capture of twenty-three Iraqi prisoners and a wealth of war matériel. The Iraqis had been attempting to shoot down coalition aircraft from their base on the oil platforms.

Naval helicopter crews also saw heated action. One day, several came under fire from small Iraqi ships, but the helicopter crews responded with machine-gun fire. They sank four ships and damaged others, which attempted to flee. Navy A-6E Intruder airplanes were summoned to attack the remaining ships.

Navy helicopter pilots also flew a variety of support missions, ferrying troops, prisoners of war, ammunition, and equipment throughout the war zone. Lt. Kelly Franke, who flew 125 combat-support missions in the Gulf, was named Naval Helicopter Pilot of the Year in 1991 for her work, which included the dangerous sea rescue of an injured diver.

Hazardous Duty

A-6E Intruders (pictured) fired on Iraqi ships that had attempted to bring down navy helicopters.

Elite Navy SEALS—SEa, Air, Land units—also made a significant contribution to the U.S. war effort. Specially trained in so-called special operations, which include espionage and infiltration, SEALs performed a host of important missions. For example, small groups of SEALs surreptitiously slipped into Iraq and Iraqi-controlled Kuwait and undertook high-risk spying activities that provided the U.S. military with important intelligence information. SEALs in enemy territory also helped direct bombing missions by coalition aircraft. In addition, SEALs conducted daring assaults on Iraqi positions. In one mission, a four-man SEAL team captured an oil well platform that was being held by 23

Iraqis. The SEALs reached the platform by helicopter and quickly subdued the Iraqi soldiers. All told, a force of 60 SEALs and 200 support personnel performed 270 missions during the Gulf War and did not suffer a single casualty.

The SEALs also served as a decoy, conducting often dangerous operations designed to make the Iraqis believe that an amphibious landing along the Kuwaiti coast was imminent. One mission for the SEALs was to clear the coastline of obstacles

A Turkey Shoot

When Iraqi troops began to flee Kuwait City, clogging the two main highways out of the city with military vehicles and stolen cars laden with Kuwaiti loot, U.S. military leaders made the decision to stop them from retreating. They reasoned that, if allowed to escape, the Iraqi army would be strong enough to continue to create problems in the region and might counterattack as soon as coalition forces left the area.

For the aviators sent out to stop the retreat, the Iraqis posed an easy target. Michael Kelly, in *Martyr's Day: Chronicle of a Small War*, recounts the air offensive:

> The attacking pilots afterward compared the experience to a turkey shoot, and to bombing the road to Daytona Beach at spring break. In the first wave, the American planes bombed the front and tail of the Iraqi convoy on the main road, so that it could move neither forward nor backward.

The desert offered no cover, and many of the vehicles the Iraqis had stolen were not capable of desert driving anyway. The pilots from the American carrier USS *Ranger* had so many targets to choose from that they extended their raids into daylight hours and had their loaders rack up whatever bombs or missiles were closest at hand rather than wait for the ship's elevators to bring up the designated ordnance. With each launch, the ship's sound system played Rossini's *William Tell Overture*.

The bombing by navy, army, and air force planes would continue through the morning of February 26, 1991.

Shattered and burned-out vehicles litter the highway after the attack on the Iraqi convoy fleeing Kuwait City.

and mines in advance of an allied amphibious assault. The work of the SEALs, along with the presence of marines on amphibious ships in the Gulf, further heightened the deception. The feint proved effective: Iraq defended the coast heavily and moved in large guns. Iraqi forces also re-mined the beaches and set out barbed wire to forestall an attack that never came.

Although marines did not make an amphibious landing on Kuwait, marines and naval personnel deployed in the Gulf found themselves in the midst of the civil war in Somalia even as Desert Storm loomed. On January 3, 1991, the U.S. embassy in Somalia requested evacuation amid civil strife, and two large helicopters loaded with marines and naval personnel were soon dispatched there. The marines landed and secured a group of evacuees. On the chopper ride to safety, a navy corpsman helped a passenger deliver a baby. The following day, choppers from a navy helicopter carrier were sent in to evacuate more than 250 foreigners from the Somali capital of Mogadishu.

Not all marine units were used as part of the elaborate amphibious-landing deception. Other marines would see intense battle. Two Marine Corps divisions encamped along the border between Saudi Arabia and Kuwait conducted frequent hazardous missions across the border even before the ground war had begun. Combat patrols passed defensive sand berms for brief attacks, often coming under intense fire. But the incursions allowed them to learn that allied air attacks had punched holes in the Iraqi defenses.

"Their Morale Is About Boot-Top Level"

Two days prior to the launch of the ground war, soldiers from the 1st Marine Division slipped into Kuwait as a heavy rainstorm drenched the area. The marines advanced twelve miles into Kuwait without being detected by the Iraqis, and then hunkered down in foxholes to await the official start of the ground war. When it came, the two marine divisions stormed into Kuwait.

They initially received little opposition, leading a marine officer to remark, "Their morale is about boot-top level."[121] However, resistance soon stiffened as the marines penetrated farther into Kuwait, and Apache helicopters from the army and jump jets and SeaCobra helicopters from the marines joined the fray. Some of the helicopters flew so low that afterward one marine officer said that he could have reached up and touched a SeaCobra's landing skids, and recalled that hot casing shells from the helicopter's cannons fell like rain on the marines. The Iraqis would lose about thirty tanks and armored vehicles in the encounter.

Although the naval missions in the Gulf War were largely successful, officers expressed frustration with administrative red tape. Despite the widespread use of computers, naval administrators found themselves overwhelmed with paperwork ranging from weather reports to equipment requisition forms to pilot mission materials. Vice Admiral Arthur jokingly said, "If Iraq had perfected a paper-seeking missile, we would have been in trouble."[122]

The navy was often overlooked by the media during the Gulf War because of the higher profile contributions of air and ground troops. Nevertheless, the war effort required the careful coordination of all service units, including the instrumental contributions of the navy ranging from medical support to offensive military operations. The war was not yet over, however.

Chapter 7

"All You Can Do Is Feel Sad for Them"

As ground troops continued to roll into Kuwait, many Iraqi soldiers were hiding in bunkers, taking cover from a continuing pounding from the air. Even the pilots dropping bombs on them had grown sympathetic to their plight. "It was a fact that Iraqi troops had committed atrocities against the people of Kuwait, but dropping bombs on soldiers incapable of defending themselves was becoming difficult for me to handle. These men were huddled together in bunkers beneath the desert floor like frightened animals, waiting to be slaughtered,"[123] writes Capt. Keith Rosenkranz. While many Iraqi soldiers were taking cover, another group went into a full retreat. Some drove heavy armor as the Iraqis attempted to save as much war machinery as possible.

To prevent the tanks from being salvaged for a counterattack or to be utilized to reinvade Iraq's neighbors once the coalition forces left the region, the United States stepped up bombing runs. Col. Hal Hornburg, a wing commander for an F-15E unit, recalled a call from Brig. Gen. Buster Glosson asking his fliers to slow the Iraqi retreat:

> He said the Iraqis were in a massive retreat out of Kuwait City, heading north with all their assets. The weather was terrible up in that region; there were heavy clouds and embedded thunderstorms. Glosson said that the other flights he had sent in had to return because of the weather. . . . I immediately called [Lt. Col. Steve] Turner and [Lt. Col. Steve] Pingel and told them to start waking up whatever guys we had who weren't out flying. I said, "Take a look at them; if they look good, send them up; if they don't look good, send them back to bed."[124]

Pilots took to the air and were astonished by what they saw. Highways leading out of Kuwait toward Iraq were clogged with retreating Iraqi forces. "I'm looking down on this road and it was like the rush hour on the Dan Ryan Expressway in Chicago. There were trucks lined up bumper to bumper. You couldn't see the road for all the traffic,"[125] said Maj. Joe Seidl.

"Situational Awareness Is a Must . . ."

Pilots began bombing the convoy of retreating troops, and soon came under intense antiaircraft fire. The cars, trucks, and armored vehicles turned off their lights, but pilots said they could still see the vehicles because of oil fires the Iraqis had set as they started their retreat.

Other pilots had trouble finding the convoy because of the ferocious thunderstorm. Maj. Larry Coleman said the storm nearly forced him to abort his mission: "I will admit it; I was very concerned. It was a vicious storm. The lightning was so white and dazzling it was almost blinding. Then it would be so black you couldn't see anything."[126]

The pilots' job was complicated by the rapid advance of U.S. and coalition ground troops, often in close proximity to enemy troops and targets. There were

A destroyed tank, one of the vehicles the retreating Iraqis attempted to save.

accidents. At one pilot briefing toward war's end, Lt. Col. Tom Rackley again cautioned the pilots to make sure they avoided shooting at coalition forces. After announcing that coalition aircraft had hit two British armored vehicles the previous evening, he said:

Situational awareness is a must out there. Make sure you know which [area] you're supposed to be in, and double-check your coordinates before you commence your target runs. We're flying at night; the weather is poor; and in the heat of battle, mistakes are going to happen. Just make sure you know where

you're at before you fire your missiles or drop your bomb. As I've said before, come off dry if there's any doubt.[127]

While in flight to their target areas, pilots checked in with controllers in the airborne AWACS to find out if coalition ground troops had entered their bombing areas. They also checked in with controllers at the Joint Surveillance Target Attack Radar System, or J-STARS, and the Airborne Battlefield Command and Con-

AWACS aircraft were used to notify pilots of allied ground troops in their bombing areas and of available enemy targets.

trol Center to be absolutely certain that no U.S. forces were within their target areas. Once cleared to proceed with their missions, pilots in turn reported to the AWACS controllers on their mission's success and the availability of more targets in the area.

"The Only Goal Left for These Men Was to Return Home"

Many pilots grew weary of bombing the retreating Iraqi forces. Captain Rosenkranz recalls: "I hated the thought of killing soldiers in the process of retreating. Six weeks of relentless bombing had not only destroyed Iraq's military equipment, it had broken the Iraqi army's will to fight. The only goal left for these men was to return home safely to their families. That was my goal, too."[128] But as they prepared for their final missions of the war, the pilots knew they had to detach themselves emotionally so that they could safely do their jobs. The assault on the retreating forces was, nevertheless, one-sided wholesale destruction, as mop-up operations discovered in the next days.

On the ground, troops were either engaged in heavy battle or overrun with surrendering Iraqis. U.S. Marines found themselves under attack as they moved toward Kuwait City and fought back against a group of tanks with helicopters and artillery fire, supported by air force and marine air strikes. At times, the battlefield was virtually obscured by smoke from the hundreds of oil well fires the Iraqis had set. Even at noon, marines could consult maps only with the aid of flashlights, and their clothing became covered with soot. Marine Maj. Bob Williams said of the Iraqis that "they fought harder than we have seen before. It really was apocalyptic."[129]

As the coalition forces made their way to Kuwait City, they picked up thousands of surrendering Iraqis. A U.S. soldier said most of the captives were not even true soldiers, but farmers and herders who had been conscripted at the point of a gun: "I felt sorry for those guys. They were real happy when they saw us, and they would be waving anything white they could find. We would motion for them to wait, or send them down the road to a prisoner pick-up point."[130] Another soldier said of the Iraqis, "They jump up like squirrels to surrender."[131] Wounded prisoners who required medical care were treated by navy medics and sent to Mobile Army Surgical Hospitals, or MASH units, as necessary. Most of the prisoners suffered from no more than dehydration and fear. U.S. Navy corpsman David Walden said of the prisoners, "Basically they just want some attention, want to know that somebody cares."[132]

"I'm as Good a Shot as Anybody"

The prisoners were herded into makeshift enemy prisoner of war camps. Most were desperate for food. Soldiers threw them MREs; at one U.S. Marine temporary POW camp, thirty-five hundred Iraqi prisoners fought each other for the packaged meals. Marines quelled the disturbance by throwing entire cardboard boxes full of MREs to the Iraqis. Although the boxes included

The defeat of Iraq left about sixty thousand Iraqi POWs in the care of the coalition.

pork dishes, forbidden under Muslim dietary rules, the near-starving captives ripped into the food and asked for more. Riots were not uncommon at the camps. At one army POW camp in Saudi Arabia, a riot broke out at 2 A.M. and five military police had to go in to restore order. One MP, Sgt. Kitty Bussell, was temporarily detained by a Saudi who said a woman had no business entering the fray. But Bussell brushed him off, saying, "I'm as good a shot as anybody."[133]

The mass surrender of Iraqi soldiers created logistical problems. U.S. forces had to transport and feed roughly sixty thousand prisoners of war in strict accordance with the terms of the Geneva Convention, which sets ground rules for treatment of captured soldiers. Capt. Kurt Snyder was a guard at one POW camp, and the Iraqi prisoners saddened him. "Poor [people]. You can't even dislike them. All you can do is feel sad for them,"[134] observes Snyder, a law school graduate assigned to guard duty at the camp in part, he says, because he had read all of the Geneva Convention.

"Cigarettes . . . Were a No-Priority"

One Convention clause required that prisoners of war be given a daily ration of cigarettes or the chance to make money in order to buy them from their captors. Lt. Gen. William G. Pagonis, a fitness advocate, did not think much of that clause and initially ignored it.

> Representatives of the International Red Cross came into my office one day to hold my feet to the fire on that point. I had already decided that this was a foolish way to spend the scarce time of my soldiers, not to mention the taxpayers' money. I told the Red Cross that as far as I was concerned, cigarettes weren't just a low priority, they were a no-priority. Rules were cited and voices were raised, but I was comfortable being stubborn on this particular issue.
>
> A few days later, my chief contracting officer, Dave Bartlett, came into my office with a military lawyer in tow. "Boss," Bartlett announced, "this guy tells me that if you don't agree to buy cigarettes for the [prisoners], *I'm* going to jail."

> The battle was lost; it was time to cut our losses. 'O.K.,' I told him. "Go out and buy the worst cigarettes you can find in the whole world. Buy enough to last thirty days, and make it clear that we aren't buying any more of the damn things."
>
> I'm told that the cigarettes were bad—very bad, in fact. But they obviously weren't bad enough. Within three weeks, Bartlett was back with more grim news: the Iraqis had gone through $80,000 worth of cigarettes in twenty days and were now demanding more.[135]

Special Forces

As the war ground to a close, U.S. Special Forces units went ahead of advancing coalition troops to subdue remaining pockets of Iraqi resistance and clear the way for the liberation of Kuwait City. Alerted by Kuwaiti citizens, one Special Forces unit captured a truck full of Iraqi soldiers and their weapons. The Iraqis were forced to lie face down on the pavement at gunpoint as they were searched and then handcuffed. The Special Forces troops then had to control an advancing crowd of Kuwaitis, who wanted to lynch the Iraqis. That scene would be replayed a number of times as the war came to an end.

The last engagement between U.S. Marines and Iraqis came on February 22. The marines encountered and destroyed two Iraqi tanks and an armored troop transport vehicle. Some of the surviving Iraqis attempted to escape, but were cornered by

the marines in a nursery. According to a marine captain, "Two battalions went through and finished them. They didn't fight much, but at least they died with their weapons in their hands."[136]

Many U.S. soldiers were deeply moved by the plight of Iraqi soldiers. Lance Cpl.

A Special Forces soldier searches a trench for hidden Iraqi troops.

"I'll Never Forget What I Saw On That Road, Ever"

Because the long-range, high-tech weapons utilized by the United States allowed U.S. soldiers to fire at the enemy from a safe distance, for many American soldiers the Persian Gulf War was more like a video game than combat. They knew what kind of damage their weapons could inflict, but usually they did not see their actual victims. Michael Kelly, a journalist who covered the Gulf War, sums up the experience in *Martyrs' Day: Chronicle of a Small War:*

> The Gulf War was an experience disconnected from itself, conducted with such speed and at such distances and with so few witnesses that it was, even for many of the people involved, an abstraction. It was difficult for the Americans, who had done their killing almost entirely from afar, to feel a connection with those they killed, or with the act of killing.

According to Kelly, the true horrors of war were apparent to the soldiers witnessing the carnage on the two highways leading out of Kuwait City toward Iraq. Those roads, on which Iraqi troops attempted to retreat with military equipment and goods they had plundered from Kuwait, made the war real. According to Kelly, the roads "were, for miles and miles, rich with the physical realities of war, glutted with the evidence of slaughter and victory. They became the great circuit board of the Gulf War, where the disconnectedness stopped."

After reviewing the wreckage, Kelly came across a camp of American soldiers and talked to its leader, Capt. Douglas Morrison. Morrison was deeply troubled by what he had seen. As related by Kelly, Morrison said:

> "It was obvious from the [enemy prisoners of war] that we took that the Iraqis had suffered from a lack of medical care, food, water. Some of them were dehydrated. They hadn't eaten in days. Some of them were kids, thirteen, fourteen, fifteen years old. Some were old men, fifty, sixty. That bothered me. Sure it did. And it bothered me when I picked up four or five dead Iraqi soldiers on the road over there. It's something you remember. I'll never forget what I saw on that road, ever."

George Cadiente recalls the emotion of taking prisoners:

> We used to say that we wouldn't take prisoners unless they came out barebutt and waving a white flag, but, oh man, some of them were crying. One guy, you know, he defecated himself. When they heard we were Marines they were certain we were going to kill them. They'd been told all sorts of bull like to join the Marine Corps you had to kill one of your own family first. Some of them wouldn't come out of their bunkers. They were curled up in there and wouldn't come out. We'd throw stones in, pretending they were grenades, and they still wouldn't come out. They'd just curl up some more. And the place was full of guns, grenades. . . . They could have fought us. When we tied their hands . . . some of them were saying, "We love you, we love you." I had one kid who couldn't have been more than sixteen. He just sat there on the ground and started crying. He was convinced I

was going to kill him. He hadn't eaten for days, you could see it. Just a kid.[137]

On February 27, 1991, President Bush announced that beginning "at midnight tonight, Eastern Standard Time, exactly 100 hours since ground operations commenced and six weeks since the start of Desert Storm, all U.S. and coalition forces will suspend offensive combat operations. It is up to Iraq whether this suspension on the part of the coalition becomes a permanent cease-fire."[138]

The Highway of Death

Troops now had the job of policing the battlefield, and soldiers got their first look at the wreckage of the allied onslaught. On the highway out of Kuwait City, soldiers saw what looked like a massive junkyard. Burned-out cars and trucks, vehicles that fleeing Iraqis had stolen from Kuwaitis, and military vehicles littered the roadway. The headlights of some abandoned vehicles were still on and the engines were still running. The charred remains of Iraqis were stiffened in other vehicles or twisted on the pavement of what journalists soon called "the highway to hell" or "the highway of death." A marine captain securing the area said of the carnage, "I wouldn't even call this a mopping-up operation."[139] A soldier viewing the scene was heard to say, "Jesus, did we really do this?"[140]

Other soldiers had become desensitized to the scene and were tired and edgy after the rapid advance of the ground attack. "The first dead Iraqi I saw was charred, and he was still sitting in the driving position, with his hands on the wheel of a truck that was still smoking. I don't know. I didn't have much feeling when I saw that. I was really tired, because for the three days of the ground war, I basically didn't sleep,"[141] recalls then-Sgt. Bill Touchette, who drove fuel trucks to support the army advance.

Like Touchette, troops became emotionally disengaged from death. He recalls one woman soldier who encountered a dead Iraqi half-buried in the sand. One of his hands was outstretched, and a wedding ring was visible. The soldier placed her hand and its wedding band next to the dead man's, and had a fellow soldier take a picture. According to Touchette, "A lot of people probably went over that way. Pretty much what we saw was no different from what you see in the movies. They're real violent and that's pretty much what we saw."[142]

"Good God, That's Murder!"

Many retreating Iraqis had plundered Kuwait and laden their escape vehicles with loot. One disabled truck carried a living room set, filing cabinets, and a large refrigerator. Washing machines, tricycles, toaster ovens, televisions, and video cassette recorders spilled across the roadway. The slaughter of the fleeing Iraqis had created tensions among air force pilots. Col. Dave Baker said that after one mission, crews took videos of their missions to senior officers, who had been waiting to see what had happened. Baker recalls:

We played the tapes and it showed [air force bombers] descending down into the weather to drop on this endless stream of vehicles. I mean, through the [night vision sights of the plane], it looked like a gigantic parking lot down there on the highway. There were people scrambling and running around down on the ground—you could actually see them—and about that time this lieutenant colonel, who was standing there watching [the tape] said, "Good God, that's murder!" Everybody turned around; then I looked at him hard and said, "Listen . . . that's not murder, that's called war. You're seeing war and all the horrors that go with it."[143]

An air force major who heard Baker speak that night said that the prominent news coverage of the highway bombing and the carnage in its wake did not merit sympathy:

A lot of those guys down there that night had looted everything they could carry; they had stereos, lamps . . . you name it, they had it. And they were in vehicles that they had stolen from the Kuwaitis. They were not soldiers trying to retreat from a battlefield, and we knew that. We would not have dropped on retreating foot soldiers; none of us would. They were a bunch of criminals escaping in stolen cars. They were

rapists, murderers, and thieves, and as far as I was concerned, they deserved what they got.[144]

Marine Gen. Walter Boomer concurred, saying of the Iraqi army, "In addition to being fairly incompetent, they were thieves as well as murderers."[145]

Continuing Hostilities

Despite the cease-fire, soldiers still faced many dangers. The hundreds of oil-well fires set by the fleeing Iraqis created a thick, sooty smoke that blocked the sun and burned throats. One Kuwaiti citizen said that attempting to breathe in the smoke-choked environment was "like taking the exhaust pipe of a diesel truck in your mouth and breathing that."[146]

Soldiers also faced a continuing military threat. Soldiers at a highway checkpoint had stopped two buses carrying Iraqi soldiers for questioning when Iraqis from one of the buses began firing on the troops. A day later, an Iraqi tank division attacked the army's 24th Infantry Division. The Iraqi unit, which had several hundred tanks and armored personnel carriers, fought fiercely in a battle that lasted close to five hours. In the end, however, the American force destroyed the unit in an action involving attack helicopters, artillery, and Abrams tanks. The entire confrontation had been something of a fluke; the Iraqis simply had been trying to get into northern Iraq. Maj. Gen. Barry R. McCaffrey, the commander of the 24th, said,

"They bumped into us going west, trying to break out across the causeway [leading to the Baghdad highway]."[147]

Pilots had an easier time of it once the cease-fire went into effect. Air Force leaders knew the pilots would experience an emotional letdown after enduring intense combat experience, so pilots were kept fly-

ing missions. Some flights were nighttime reconnaissance missions to be on the lookout for possible Scud attacks against Israel. But during daytime runs over Iraq, pilots

A soldier walks past dead Iraqis as oil-well fires in the background fill the sky with thick, black smoke.

largely did whatever they wanted. Some inspected the hot spots that had plagued them with antiaircraft fire during the war; others flew low simply to feel the exhilaration of low-altitude flight.

Low-Fliers

When General Schwarzkopf met with his Iraqi counterpart at Safwan, Iraq, on March 3, 1991, to complete a formal cease-fire agreement, F-15E Strike Eagle pilots made low runs over the area. "We were to go in as a two-ship at thirty-minute intervals, with the burner lit to make us louder, and fly by at 300 feet. It was a little bit of psychological warfare just to remind the Iraqis who was boss. I did that a couple times and there were several guys who went quite a bit lower,"[148] one pilot recalls. Pilots even flew low over Baghdad, one pilot making a low pass over a statue of Saddam Hussein while reaching supersonic speed.

Another pilot recalled showing off near Iraq's equivalent of the U.S. Air Force Academy:

> I wanted to put on a real show for those guys. So we made a low pass and they came outside and waved—just like all the Iraqis did when we made low passes —they loved it. Then I came back around and lit the burner and went screaming right in front of them. There are about twenty guys standing outside this hangar and they are all waving at me, enjoying the air show. Then I looked out in front and there

are telephone wires right in my face. I pulled six and one-half Gs and stood it on its tail. Somehow I missed the wires; I don't like to think about what would have happened if I had not seen those wires.[149]

A Deadly Loophole

The pilots described such missions as fun, but the enjoyment soon melted away as a result of a concession made to the Iraqis during the cease-fire talks. The U.S.-led coalition initially demanded that the Iraqis fly no aircraft whatsoever, but the Iraqi general pointed out that the allies had torn up roads, bridges, and communications to such an extent that government officials would be unable to get around without helicopters. Schwarzkopf explains the agreement that was reached:

> It appeared to me to be a legitimate request. And given that the Iraqis had agreed to all our requests, I didn't feel it was unreasonable to grant one of theirs. "As long as it is not over the part we are in, that is absolutely no problem. So we will let the helicopters fly. That is a very important point, and I want to make sure it's recorded, that military helicopters can fly over Iraq. Not fighters, not bombers."[150]

American pilots would soon become angered over violations of the agreement. One day pilots were flying a mission to enforce the so-called no-fly restriction when they saw

During the cease-fire negotiations, General Norman Schwarzkopf (left) agreed to Iraq's request to use helicopters.

a convoy of Kurds, an ethnic minority long subject to Iraqi persecution, fleeing from Iraqi soldiers and headed for sanctuary in Turkey. One pilot remembers the scene:

> Then we look down and there are waves of helicopters that have come off Al Fathah. They are Hinds, Russian gunships, carrying machine guns and rockets, and while we're looking down there in horror, they begin flying in a circle over those people, firing directly into them. We called AWACS and told them what was happening and requested permission to attack the heli- copters. "We'll get back to you," they said. I mean, it is so bad down there, you don't even want to look. It is carnage; they are firing into innocent civilians—women and children. Finally, after what seemed like hours, AWACS comes back, "Negative on your request. You cannot fire upon helicopters unless they deliberately fire upon you."[151]

Pilots did what they could to help. Some flew directly above and below the helicopters in an attempt to create air turbulence that might break helicopter rotors or otherwise force the helicopters down. Others focused lasers on the helicopter pilots in an attempt to blind them.

One Strike Eagle crew, a pilot and a weapons system officer, deliberately flew near helicopter gunfire. "Hey, they are shooting at me now; the bullets just went by our canopy. Are we cleared to return fire?"[152] a pilot radioed to the AWACS controllers. When the controllers asked if the helicopter actually had its guns trained on the plane, the pilot had to admit that it did not. "Then you cannot fire at them. Acknowledge,"[153] came the reply. The pilot was eventually able to force the helicopter down by creating air turbulence but knew his efforts were of little long-term significance. Pilots began to admit similar skepticism about their victory in the Gulf War:

After the war, while I was waiting to come home, I wrote several letters to kids in Texas who had written me. I told them that what we had done in that war might sound great, but it was just a Band-Aid approach. Try to realize that we were just temporary actors on the stage in a never-ending play. We didn't stop anything. The fighting and bloodshed over there is never ending. It will go on, and on, and on.[154]

"We'll Never See Anything Like This"

As U.S. and coalition allies rolled into Kuwait City on February 27, residents of the liberated city treated the troops to a flag-waving, heroes' welcome. The Kuwaitis cheered the soldiers and yelled their thanks. "Thank you, USA," some shouted. Another said, "At last you did it! God bless Bush!",[155] a reference to President Bush's resolve to force Iraqi troops from Kuwait. Marine Lt. Gen. Walter E. Boomer was touched by the welcome, as hundreds of Kuwaitis in cars and on foot swirled by the advancing convoy of troops. "We'll never see anything like this in our lifetimes. Makes you appreciate freedom, doesn't it?"[156] Boomer said.

However, the welcome troops received in Kuwait City was small compared to what was in store for troops when they got home. By mid-March, thousands of soldiers were returning home everyday, greeted by flag-waving rallies and parades. On March 28, an estimated 50,000 people lined the pier at the navy's port in Norfolk, Virginia, to greet returning crew members aboard the *San Jacinto, South Carolina, Biddle, Thomas Hart, Seattle, John F. Kennedy,* and *Wisconsin.*

On April 17, the *Iwo Jima* docked in Morehead City, North Carolina, where school children had been given the day off to welcome returning marines. Thousands of children and adults lined the route of the troops back to Camp Lejune, cheering wildly.

After the hoopla died down, however, soldiers moved on with their lives. Although some stayed in the service, many decided to leave. The military encouraged the exodus, as it sought to continue force-size reductions that had begun prior to the Gulf War. Under the Early Transition Program, soldiers could be honorably discharged even before their tours of duty had been completed.

Captain Keith Rosenkranz felt it was time for a change and left the air force shortly after the war's end. "I had accomplished everything I wanted as a fighter pilot, and the fact that I had spent twenty-one of the past twenty-four months away from my family convinced me it was time to move in a new direction,"[157] says Rosenkranz, who now is an airline pilot.

Some soldiers, like Sgt. Bill Touchette, left the service in part because of a desire to return to the United States. Touchette's unit had been stationed in Germany prior to Desert Shield and Desert Storm.

Touchette is now a letter carrier for the postal service.

While most Gulf veterans who left the service have gone on to relatively quiet lives, at least one has achieved a level of notoriety. Timothy McVeigh was an army sergeant in the Gulf War, a gunner on a

Well-wishers crowd the streets during a parade in New York City to welcome the Gulf War veterans home.

A tuberculosis-stricken Gulf War veteran, one of over a hundred thousand who suffer from Gulf War Syndrome.

Bradley fighting vehicle. McVeigh made his first kill on the first day of the ground war, hitting an Iraqi in the neck from a distance of roughly 1,100 yards—the equivalent of eleven football fields. He later destroyed an Iraqi machine gun emplacement and forced the surrender of 30 Iraqis. McVeigh received an Army Commendation Medal for his actions. Shortly after the war, he left the army with an honorable discharge and soon be-

came enmeshed with antigovernment groups. On April 19, 1995, the Alfred P. Murrah Federal Building in Oklahoma City was bombed, killing 168 and injuring another 500. Two days later, McVeigh was formally charged in the bombing. On June 2, 1997, a federal jury found him guilty of murder, and on June 13, 1997, recommended that McVeigh be executed for his role in the attack.

Although the Gulf War call-ups made clear that armed forces reserve units would play a more active role in future conflicts, many reservists have stayed in the reserves. Some ten years after the Gulf War, Sgt. John Grifka still serves, knowing that he could be called upon at anytime a military need arises. Grifka says he noticed a decrease in the number of new reservists immediately following the Gulf War, but says sign-ups subsequently increased as people were attracted by the financial and educational benefits of reserve service.

The majority of returning Gulf War veterans resumed their lives without incident, but roughly 110,000 returned from the war and began to complain of joint pain, headaches, fatigue, memory loss, and rashes. The collection of maladies has come to be called Gulf War Syndrome, but doctors and scientists still do not know what triggered the illnesses. Possible chemical exposure is one explanation.

Although officials have said Iraq did not use its store of chemical weapons, U.S. planes bombed Iraqi chemical weapons facilities, and U.S. ground troops blew up Iraqi ammunition stores, some of which contained chemical weapons. Those actions may have released the poisons, leading to soldiers' illnesses, but a true cause of Gulf War Syndrome may never be known.

Most soldiers returned from the war without injury, and a majority have been untouched by Gulf War Syndrome. Nevertheless, they were marked by their experience of war. As Rosenkranz sums up:

Years have passed since the end of the Persian Gulf War, and a day doesn't go by that I'm not reminded of the experience. . . . Looking back, I would have been extremely disappointed if our unit had been left behind during the initial deployment. On the other hand, the war stole a part of my life that can never be replaced, and left me with a burden of guilt that will remain in my heart forever. I felt compassion for the people of Kuwait and everything they went through. I also felt compassion for the people of Iraq. Many of them were innocent victims of Saddam Hussein's brutality, and I feel bad for any additional suffering that I personally may have caused them. Time has a wonderful way of healing wounds, and I hope I have an opportunity to visit with the people of Iraq some day, under circumstances different than my last visit.[158]

★ Notes ★

Introduction: "This Will Not Stand"

1. Quoted in Peter David, *Triumph in the Desert: The Challenge, the Fighting, the Legacy*. New York: Random House, 1991, p. 46.
2. Quoted in Stars and Stripes Staff, "Troops Turn Thoughts Inward as Ground War Looms Closer," *Stars and Stripes Desert Storm January 17–February 28, 1991: A Commemorative Edition*, p. 63.
3. Quoted in Stars and Stripes Staff, "Troops Turn Thoughts," p. 63.
4. Quoted in David, *Triumph*, p. 116.

Chapter 1: "The Army Is Just Like an Anthill"

5. Author's interviews with Sgt. Bill Touchette, Fort Worth, TX, February 8–February 13, 2000.
6. Author's interview with Sgt. John Grifka, Fort Worth, TX, February 21, 2000.
7. Interviews with Touchette.
8. Interviews with Touchette.
9. "Getting to the Desert: Deployment and Selective Callup Lessons—Desert Shield, 90-11," Center for Army Lessons Learned. http://call.army.mi/call/newsltrs/90-11.

10. Quoted in John Sack, *Company C: The Real War in Iraq*. New York: William Morrow, 1995, p. 16.
11. Interviews with Touchette.
12. Quoted in Sack, *Company C*, p. 7.
13. Interviews with Touchette.

Chapter 2: "It was Home"

14. Lt. Gen. William G. Pagonis and Jeffrey L. Cruikshank, *Moving Mountains: Lessons in Leadership and Logistics from the Gulf War*. Boston: Harvard Business School Press, 1992, p. 8.
15. Interviews with Touchette.
16. Interviews with Touchette.
17. Interviews with Touchette.
18. Quoted in Maj. Gen. Jeanne Holm, USAF (Ret.), *Women in the Military: An Unfinished Revolution*. Rev. ed. Novato, CA: Presidio Press, 1992, p. 455.
19. Quoted in Thomas B. Allen, F. Clifton Berry, and Norman Polmar, *CNN War in the Gulf: From the Invasion of Kuwait to the Day of Victory and Beyond*. Atlanta: Turner Publishing, 1991, p. 96.
20. Quoted in David E. Jones, *Women Warriors: A History*. Washington, DC: Brassey's, 1997, p. 245.
21. Quoted in Carsten Stroud, *Iron Bravo:*

Hearts, Minds and Sergeants in the U.S. Army. New York: Bantam, 1995, p. 118.

22. Pagonis and Cruikshank, *Moving Mountains*, p. 128.

23. Pagonis and Cruikshank, *Moving Mountains*, p. 129.

24. Interviews with Touchette.

25. Interviews with Touchette.

26. Quoted in David, *Triumph*, p. 150.

27. Interviews with Touchette.

Chapter 3: "I Would Trust Her to Cover My Back . . ."

28. Quoted in Holm, *Women in the Military*, p. 470.

29. Quoted in Stroud, *Iron Bravo*, p. 92.

30. Quoted in Andrea Gross, "Women Under Fire," *Women in the Military*, E. A. Blacksmith, ed. New York: H. W. Wilson, 1992, p. 81.

31. Stephen M. Duncan, *Citizen Warriors: America's National Guard and Reserve Forces & the Politics of National Security.* Novato, CA: Presidio Press, 1997, pp. 27–28.

32. Duncan, *Citizen Warriors*, p. 77.

33. Quoted in Linda Bird Francke, *Ground Zero: The Gender Wars in the Military.* New York: Simon & Schuster, 1997, p. 141.

34. Quoted in Francke, *Ground Zero*, p. 136.

35. Quoted in Brian Mitchell, *Women in the Military: Flirting with Disaster.* Washington, DC: Regnery, 1998, p. 204.

36. Quoted in Francke, *Ground Zero*, p. 113.

37. Quoted in Francke, *Ground Zero*, p. 113.

38. Quoted in Mitchell, *Women in the Military*, p. 200.

39. Quoted in Mitchell, *Women in the Military*, p. 203.

40. Quoted in Mitchell, *Women in the Military*, pp. 203–204.

41. Quoted in Francke, *Ground Zero*, p. 145.

42. Quoted in Holm, *Women in the Military*, p. 443.

43. Quoted in Holm, *Women in the Military*, p. 443.

44. Quoted in Francke, *Ground Zero*, p. 131.

45. Quoted in Stroud, *Iron Bravo*, p. 115.

46. Quoted in C. D. B. Bryan and Sygma Photographers, *In the Eye of Desert Storm: Photographers of the Gulf War.* New York: Harry N. Abrams, 1991, p. 53.

47. Quoted in Holm, *Women in the Military*, p. 460.

48. Quoted in Francke, *Ground Zero*, p. 13.

49. Quoted in Holm, *Women in the Military*, p. 451.

50. Quoted in Holm, *Women in the Military*, p. 451.

51. Quoted in Jones, *Women Warriors*, p. 245.

52. Quoted in Holm, *Women in the Military*, p. 453.

53. Quoted in Holm, *Women in the Military*, p. 455.

54. Quoted in Holm, *Women in the Military*, p. 453.

55. Quoted in Holm, *Women in the Military*, p. 444.
56. Quoted in Francke, *Ground Zero*, p. 77.
57. Quoted in Francke, *Ground Zero*, p. 96.
58. Quoted in Francke, *Ground Zero*, p. 92.
59. Quoted in Holm, *Women in the Military*, p. 458.
60. Quoted in Francke, *Ground Zero*, p. 99.
61. Quoted in Holm, *Women in the Military*, p. 458.
62. Quoted in Francke, *Ground Zero*, p. 99.
63. Quoted in Holm, *Women in the Military*, p. 459.

Chapter 4: The Thunder in Desert Storm

64. Quoted in William L. Smallwood, *Strike Eagle: Flying the F-15E in the Gulf War*. Washington, DC: Brassey's, 1994, p. 3.
65. Quoted in Smallwood, *Strike Eagle*, p. 58.
66. Capt. Keith Rosenkranz, *Vipers in the Storm: Diary of a Gulf War Fighter Pilot*. New York: McGraw-Hill, 1999, p. 143.
67. Quoted in Smallwood, *Strike Eagle*, p. 73.
68. Rosenkranz, *Vipers*, p. 109.
69. Quoted in Smallwood, *Strike Eagle*, p. 62.
70. Quoted in Smallwood, *Strike Eagle*, p. 64.
71. Quoted in Rosenkranz, *Vipers*, p. 148.
72. Quoted in Rosenkranz, *Vipers*, p. 149.
73. Quoted in Rosenkranz, *Vipers*, p. 150.
74. Quoted in Rosenkranz, *Vipers*, p. 151.
75. Quoted in Rosenkranz, *Vipers*, p. 169.
76. Quoted in Smallwood, *Strike Eagle*, pp. 87–88.
77. Quoted in Francke, *Ground Zero*, p. 101.
78. Quoted in Allen, Berry, and Polmar, *CNN War in the Gulf*, p. 118.
79. Quoted in Gregory Jaynes, "It Looks Like *Star Wars*," in David, *Triumph*, p. 144.
80. Quoted in Jaynes, "It Looks Like *Star Wars*," p. 144.
81. Quoted in Jaynes, "It Looks Like *Star Wars*," p. 144.
82. Quoted in Allen, Berry, and Polmar, *CNN War in the Gulf*, p. 124.
83. Quoted in Allen, Berry, and Polmar, *CNN War in the Gulf*, p. 125.
84. Quoted in Allen, Berry, and Polmar, *CNN War in the Gulf*, p. 126.
85. Quoted in Smallwood, *Strike Eagle*, p. 77.
86. Quoted in Smallwood, *Strike Eagle*, p. 73.
87. Quoted in Smallwood, *Strike Eagle*, p. 75.
88. Quoted in Allen, Berry, and Polmar, *CNN War in the Gulf*, p. 147.
89. Quoted in Allen, Berry, and Polmar, *CNN War in the Gulf*, p. 203.

Chapter 5: "If I Don't Get to Kill Somebody Soon . . ."

90. Quoted in Allen, Berry, and Polmar, *CNN War in the Gulf*, pp. 182–83.
91. Pagonis and Cruikshank, *Moving Mountains*, p. 138.

92. Pagonis and Cruikshank, *Moving Mountains*, pp. 145–46.

93. Quoted in Stroud, *Iron Bravo*, p. 134.

94. Quoted in Allen, Berry, and Polmar, *CNN War in the Gulf*, p. 183.

95. Quoted in Sack, *Company C*, pp. 64–66.

96. Quoted in Stroud, *Iron Bravo*, p. 178.

97. Quoted in Stroud, *Iron Bravo*, p. 178.

98. Interviews with Touchette.

99. Quoted in Sack, *Company C*, p. 110.

100. Quoted in Stroud, *Iron Bravo*, pp. 228–29.

101. Quoted in Stroud, *Iron Bravo*, p. 217.

102. Quoted in Sack, *Company C*, pp. 144–45.

103. Quoted in John Fialka, "The Climactic Tank Battle," in David, *Triumph*, p. 166.

104. Quoted in Fialka, "The Climactic Tank Battle," p. 166.

105. Quoted in Fialka, "The Climactic Tank Battle," p. 166.

106. Quoted in Fialka, "The Climactic Tank Battle," p. 166.

107. Quoted in Fialka, "The Climactic Tank Battle," p. 167.

108. Interviews with Touchette.

Chapter 6: "The Air Force Can't Do Everything"

109. Quoted in Associated Press, "Missouri's Guns Signal Fiercer Navy Role," *Stars and Stripes Desert Storm January 17–February 28, 1991*, p. 40.

110. Quoted in Allen, Berry, and Polmar, *CNN War in the Gulf*, p. 104.

111. Duncan, *Citizen Warriors*, p. 101.

112. Quoted in Cox News Services, "Navy Medic Assigned to Marines to Receive War's 1st Purple Heart," *Stars and Stripes Desert Storm January 17–February 28, 1991*, p. 21.

113. Bryan and Sygma Photographers, *In the Eye*, p. 74.

114. Quoted in Allen, Berry, and Polmar, *CNN War in the Gulf*, pp. 165–66.

115. Quoted in Associated Press, "Missouri's Guns," p. 40.

116. Quoted in Associated Press, "Missouri's Guns," p. 40.

117. Quoted in Associated Press, "Missouri's Guns," p. 40.

118. Quoted in Allen, Berry, and Polmar, *CNN War in the Gulf*, p. 166.

119. Quoted in Allen, Berry, and Polmar, *CNN War in the Gulf*, p. 170.

120. Quoted in Cox Newspapers and *Washington Post*, "Details Emerge in Daring Rescue of Navy Pilot," *Stars and Stripes Desert Storm January 17–February 28, 1991*, p. 24.

121. Quoted in David, *Triumph*, p. 84.

122. Quoted in Allen, Berry, and Polmar, *CNN War in the Gulf*, p. 177.

Chapter 7: "All You Can Do Is Feel Sad for Them"

123. Rosenkranz, *Vipers*, p. 253.

124. Quoted in Smallwood, *Strike Eagle*, p. 188.

125. Quoted in Smallwood, *Strike Eagle*, p. 189.

126. Quoted in Smallwood, *Strike Eagle*, p. 191.
127. Quoted in Rosenkranz, *Vipers*, p. 289.
128. Rosenkranz, *Vipers*, p. 289.
129. Quoted in Philip M. Taylor, *War and the Media: Propaganda and Persuasion in the Gulf War*. Manchester: Manchester University Press, 1992, p. 256.
130. Interviews with Touchette.
131. Quoted in Taylor, *War and the Media*, p. 238.
132. Quoted in Colin Smith, "Surrender and Retreat of a Broken Army," in David, *Triumph*, p. 175.
133. Quoted in Holm, *Women in the Military*, p. 447.
134. Quoted in Smith, "Surrender and Retreat," p. 175.
135. Pagonis and Cruikshank, *Moving Mountains*, pp. 10–11.
136. Quoted in Smith, "Surrender and Retreat," p. 175.
137. Quoted in Smith, "Surrender and Retreat," p. 175.
138. Quoted in Allen, Barry, and Polmar, *CNN War in the Gulf*, pp. 213–14.
139. Quoted in Smith, "Surrender and Retreat," p. 175.
140. Quoted in Taylor, *War and the Media*, p. 258.
141. Interviews with Touchette.
142. Interviews with Touchette.
143. Quoted in Smallwood, *Strike Eagle*, p. 192.
144. Quoted in Smallwood, *Strike Eagle*, p. 192.
145. Quoted in Taylor, *War and the Media*, p. 257.
146. Quoted in Allen, Barry, and Polmar, *CNN War in the Gulf*, p. 221.
147. Quoted in Allen, Barry, and Polmar, *CNN War in the Gulf*, p. 215.
148. Quoted in Smallwood, *Strike Eagle*, pp. 196–97.
149. Quoted in Smallwood, *Strike Eagle*, p. 197.
150. Quoted in Smallwood, *Strike Eagle*, p. 200.
151. Quoted in Smallwood, *Strike Eagle*, p. 200.
152. Quoted in Smallwood, *Strike Eagle*, p. 201.
153. Quoted in Smallwood, *Strike Eagle*, p. 201.
154. Quoted in Smallwood, *Strike Eagle*, p. 202.

Epilogue: "We'll Never See Anything Like This"

155. Quoted in John King, Associated Press, "Amid ruin, Kuwait hails liberators," *Stars and Stripes Desert Storm January 17–February 28, 1991*, p. 92.
156. Quoted in John King, "Amid ruin," p. 92.
157. Rosenkranz, *Vipers*, p. 306.
158. Rosenkranz, *Vipers*, p. 307.

☆ Glossary ☆

AAA: Also known as "triple-A," the acronym stands for antiaircraft artillery but also includes any ground-to-air gunfire.

Abrams: The M1A1 tank, weighing 65 tons and capable of speeds of up to 60 miles per hour.

Apache: AH-64 helicopter gunship.

AWACS: Airborne Warning and Control System aircraft used as command-and-control aircraft. The planes are characterized by a large, revolving radar dome on their fuselage.

BDU: Battle dress uniform.

Bradley: Lightly armored infantry fighting vehicle used to engage enemy troops and transport infantry.

chocolate chips: Nickname given to desert camouflage design on soldiers' battle dress uniforms.

Cobra: Helicopter gunship.

EPWs: Gulf War abbreviation for enemy prisoners of war.

GPS: Global Positioning System, a satellite-based navigation system that allows soldiers to determine where they are in an often featureless desert.

Humvee: The military's successor to the Jeep, more formally known as high-mobility, multipurpose wheeled vehicles.

MREs: The acronym for food packets developed by the military known as meals, ready to eat.

Scud: Soviet-designed, often erratic missile used by Iraq. Troops feared that the missiles had been fitted with chemical weapons.

Tomahawk: Computer-guided missile utilized by the Navy to strike targets deep inside Iraq.

Warthog: Nickname for the A-10 Thunderbolt aircraft.

☆ Chronology of Events ☆

1990

August 2: Iraq invades Kuwait; the United Nations responds by passing Resolution 660, which condemns the invasion and demands Iraq's immediate withdrawal.

August 6: Secretary of Defense Richard Cheney and Gen. H. Norman Schwarzkopf confer with Saudi King Fahd Ibn Abdel-Aziz about sending U.S. military forces to defend against a possible Iraqi invasion of Saudi Arabia; UN passes Resolution 661, placing a trade embargo on Iraq.

August 7: President George Bush launches Operation Desert Shield; U.S. forces begin to deploy to Saudi Arabia.

August 9: First U.S. troops arrive in Saudi Arabia.

August 27: U.S. Army's heavy gear begins to arrive in Saudi Arabia.

November 29: UN adopts Resolution 678, which sets January 15, 1991, as the deadline for Iraqi withdrawal from Kuwait and authorizes the use of force if Iraq does not comply.

December 22: Iraqi dictator Saddam Hussein announces his country will not leave Kuwait, and that if attacked, Iraq will use chemical weapons.

1991

January 9: Secretary of State James Baker meets in Geneva, Switzerland, with Iraqi foreign minister Tariq Aziz in a final attempt to reach a peaceful resolution to the Gulf crisis.

January 12: U.S. Senate votes 52–47 to authorize President Bush to use force to make Iraq comply with the UN resolutions; U.S. House of Representatives votes 250–183 to allow Bush to use force.

January 17: U.S. and coalition forces launch an unrelenting air attack against Iraq.

January 18: Iraq launches its first Scud missile at Israel.

February 22: President Bush gives Iraq a final warning to withdraw or risk ground attack.

February 24: U.S. and coalition forces begin ground attack against Iraq and Iraqi positions in Kuwait.

February 27: Just 100 hours after it began, the ground war results in the liberation of Kuwait; a temporary cease-fire is put in place.

March 3: Schwarzkopf meets Iraqi generals to make formal cease-fire arrangements.

April 6: Iraq accepts all UN resolutions regarding its takeover of Kuwait.

☆ For Further Reading ☆

Books

Fred Bratman, *War in the Persian Gulf.* Brookfield, CT: The Millbrook Press, 1991. Examines the complicated political tensions in the Persian Gulf region and provides an overview of the Persian Gulf War.

Kathlyn Gay and Martin Gay, *Persian Gulf War.* New York: Twenty-First Century Books, 1996. Offers a broad overview of the Persian Gulf War.

Zachary Kent, *The Persian Gulf War: "The Mother of All Battles."* Hillside, NJ Enslow Publishers Inc., 1994. Provides a broad look at the Persian Gulf War, its causes, and a glimpse at the lives of the troops who served in it.

John Pimlott, *Middle East: A Background to the Crisis.* New York: Gloucester Press, 1991. Examines long-running tensions in the Persian Gulf region and offers an overview of the simmering conflict between Arabs and Israelis.

Carol Wekesser and Matthew Polesetsky, eds., *Women in the Military.* San Diego: Greenhaven Press, 1991. Provides a sweeping look at both the benefits and drawbacks of women serving in the armed forces.

Websites

Gulf War History Resources (www.snow-crest.net/jmike/gulfwarmil.html). A wide range of information and links to sites regarding all aspects of the Gulf War.

Information Resource Centre, Canadian Forces College (www.cfcsc.dnd.ca/links/milhist/gw.html). Contains a vast wealth of information and links to sites dedicated to issues concerning the Persian Gulf War.

Naval Health Research Center (www.nhrc.navy.mil/Pubs/Subject/06.html). Provides links to abstracts of studies conducted by the Naval Health Research Center, many of which deal with illnesses that some believe are related to service in the Persian Gulf War.

Persian Gulf War Veterans' Information & Referral Center (www.grapevine.net/~Krogers/). A wide range of information and links for Persian Gulf veterans and students.

★ Works Consulted ★

Books

Thomas B. Allen, F. Clifton Berry, and Norman Polmar, *CNN War in the Gulf: From the Invasion of Kuwait to the Day of Victory and Beyond.* Atlanta: Turner Publishing, 1991. A comprehensive overview of the events leading to the Gulf War and the conduct of the war.

E. A. Blacksmith, ed., *Women in the Military.* New York: H. W. Wilson, 1992. A collection of articles and book excerpts analyzing the benefits and drawbacks of allowing women to serve in the military.

Daniel P. Bolger, *Savage Peace: Americans at War in the 1990s.* Novato, CA: Presidio Press, 1995. A broad look at American peace-keeping activities during the 1990s.

C. D. B. Bryan and Sygma Photographers, *In the Eye of Desert Storm: Photographers of the Gulf War.* New York: Harry N. Abrams, 1991. Rich, sometimes haunting photographs from the Gulf War, with text by the photographers who shot them.

Peter David, *Triumph in the Desert: The Challenge, the Fighting, the Legacy.* New York: Random House, 1991. Lavishly illustrated photo history of the Gulf War, with a textual analysis of the war, its causes, and aftermath.

Stephen M. Duncan, *Citizen Warriors: America's National Guard and Reserve Forces & the Politics of National Security.* Novato, CA: Presidio Press, 1997. A thorough modern history of America's reserve and National Guard forces, including a detailed analysis of reserve contributions in the Persian Gulf War.

James F. Dunnigan and Albert A. Nofi, *Dirty Little Secrets: Military Information You're Not Supposed to Know.* New York: William Morrow and Company, 1990. A compilation of often unusual military arcana, including characteristics of modern weaponry.

Linda Bird Francke, *Ground Zero: The Gender Wars in the Military.* New York: Simon & Schuster, 1997. A thorough examination of the problems and opportunities for women in the military, including a detailed discussion of the role of women in the Persian Gulf War.

Norman Friedman, *Desert Victory: The War for Kuwait.* Annapolis: Naval Institute Press, 1991. A comprehensive analysis of the Persian Gulf War and the weapons used to wage it.

Maj. Gen. Jeanne Holm, USAF (Ret.), *Women in the Military: An Unfinished Revolution.* Novato, CA: Presidio Press, 1992. A thorough and intriguing look at the issues presented by women in the military, with a fascinating examination of the role played by women in the Persian Gulf War.

David E. Jones, *Women Warriors: A History.* Washington, DC: Brassey's, 1997. A broad historical overview of women in arms, with stories of women combatants from the Gulf War.

Michael Kelly, *Martyrs' Day: Chronicle of a Small War.* New York: Vintage Books, 1994. A reporter's-eye view of the carnage and suffering of war.

John R. MacArthur, *Second Front: Censorship and Propaganda in the Gulf War.* New York: Hill and Wang, 1992. A look at government censorship activities and media complicity during the Gulf War.

Brian Mitchell, *Women in the Military: Flirting with Disaster.* Washington, DC: Regnery, 1998. A detractor takes aim at women in the military, arguing that the U.S. military experience—including that of the Persian Gulf War—demonstrates that women should not serve in the armed forces.

Lt. Gen. William G. Pagonis with Jeffrey L. Cruikshank, *Moving Mountains: Lessons in Leadership and Logistics from the Gulf War.* Boston: Harvard Business School Press, 1992. An intriguing first-hand look at the monumental task of deploying and bringing home American troops and their equipment.

Capt. Keith Rosenkranz, *Vipers in the Storm: Diary of a Gulf War Fighter Pilot.* New York: McGraw-Hill, 1999. A gripping and moving look at the Persian Gulf War through the eyes of an air force pilot.

John Sack, *Company C: The Real War in Iraq.* New York: William Morrow, 1995. A fast-paced look at the fear and terror faced by troops in the Persian Gulf War.

William L. Smallwood, *Strike Eagle: Flying the F-15E in the Gulf War.* Washington, DC: Brassey's, 1994. A gripping account of the lives of fighter pilots during the Gulf War.

Carsten Stroud, *Iron Bravo: Hearts, Minds, and Sergeants in the U.S. Army.* New York: Bantam, 1995. A moving and engaging portrait of the life of infantry soldiers, focusing on their experience in the Persian Gulf War.

Philip M. Taylor, *War and the Media: Propaganda and Persuasion in the Gulf War.* Manchester: Manchester University Press, 1992. A thorough analysis of attempts by both coalition governments and Iraq to influence public opinion during the Gulf War through propaganda.

Susan Besze Wallace, *Love & War: 250 Years of Wartime Love Letters.* Arlington, TX: The Summit Publishing Group, 1997. An intriguing collection of wartime love letters, ranging from the Revolutionary War to the Persian Gulf War.

Periodicals

Stars and Stripes Staff, *Stars and Stripes Desert Storm January 17–February 28, 1991: A Commemorative Edition.*

Websites

Federation of American Scientists (FAS) Military Analysis Network (www.fas.org/man/dod101/ops/desert_storm.htm). Articles, reports, and links covering the breadth of the Persian Gulf War.

U.S. Army Center for Army Lessons Learned (http://call.army.mi/call/newsltrs). A variety of newsletters outlining lessons learned from the experience of the U.S. Army during Desert Shield and Desert Storm.

☆ Index ☆

★ Picture Credits ★

Cover photo: © Peter Turnley/Corbis

© Aero Graphics, Inc./Corbis, 49, 50, 54, 62

© AFP/Corbis, 44, 53, 106, 108

© John H. Clark/Corbis, 76

© Corbis, 18, 36, 37, 45, 47, 65, 78, 79 (both), 82, 84, 85, 88, 93, 98

© Yves Debay; The Military Picture Library/Corbis, 31

© Bill Gentile/Corbis, 11, 15, 32

© George Hall/Corbis, 94

Imapress/Archive Photos, 20

Reuters/Mark Cardwell/Archive Photos, 107

Reuters/Andy Clark/Archive Photos, 64, 67, 104

Reuters/Richard Ellis/Archive Photos, 57

Reuters/Yves Herman/Archive Photos, 61

Reuters/Santiago Lyon/Archive Photos, 102

Reuters/Win McNamee/Archive Photos, 27, 34

Reuters/Frederic Neema/Archive Photos, 72

Martha Schierholz, 24

© David Turnley/Corbis, 12, 13, 21, 23, 25, 39, 41, 81

© Peter Turnley/Corbis, 7, 9, 10, 70, 73, 89, 92, 96

★ About the Author ★

Geoffrey A. Campbell is a freelance writer in Fort Worth, Texas, where he lives with his wife, Linda, his twins, Mackenzie and Kirby, two cats, and a dog. His work frequently appears in the Fort Worth Star-Telegram, and he has been published regularly in the World Book Yearbook. This is his second book; his first, *The Pentagon Papers: National Security Versus the Public's Right to Know*, was published by Lucent Books in 2000. Mr. Campbell is a certified religious education teacher, a frequent volunteer in the Fort Worth Independent School District, and is active in coaching youth sports.